全世界最暢銷的年曆
沒有窮理查，就沒有查理．蒙格

窮理查的智慧

Poor Richard's Almanack

美國國會圖書館推薦，「塑造美國」的88本書之一
哈佛商學院、華頓商學院 必讀書目

富蘭克林的格言，比商學院學到的東西更有益。
——波克夏公司副董事長 查理．蒙格

如果還沒有讀過《窮理查的智慧》，不能說你已經掌握只有兩百多年歷史的美國迅速崛起的奧秘。
——《紐約時報》書評

班傑明．富蘭克林最早在《窮理查的智慧》中推廣的那些樸實的美德，持續鼓舞一代又一代的人盡忠於我們的國家。這些美德是：自力更生、自我提升、敢於冒險的價值觀，自我激勵、自律自制、努力工作的價值觀，節儉、勇於承擔責任的價值觀。
——美國前總統 歐巴馬

Benjamin Franklin
班傑明．富蘭克林／著
王奕偉／譯

前言

美國國會圖書館推薦

哈佛商學院、華頓商學院 必讀書目

富蘭克林這本著作風靡全球，成為除了《聖經》以外最暢銷的書……在《財富之路》一文內，富蘭克林清楚簡單地說明，勤奮、小心、儉樸、穩健是致富之核心態度。——知名企業家 李嘉誠

班傑明・富蘭克林（Benjamin Franklin，1706～1790），美國開國元勳之一、功勳卓著的政治家、美國獨立運動的領導者、民主精神的締造者、《獨立宣言》的起草者。此外，他還是一位著名的出版家、作家、社會實業家、慈善家，深受全世界人民的愛戴，被美國《大西洋月刊》評為「影響美國的100位人物」的第6名。

《窮理查的智慧》（Poor Richard's Almanack）是班傑明・富蘭克林發表的年鑑，為了其出版的目的，他在書中採用「窮理查」或是「理查・桑德斯」（Richard Saunders）的假名，描繪關於生活、理財、致富的智慧箴言。這本書從1733年到1758年持續出版，以箴言的形式呈現富蘭克林的成功經驗與人生感悟，在美國殖民地時代是一本暢銷的小冊子，內容包括：季節性天氣預報、實用家務提示、猜謎遊戲，以及其他娛樂，當年出版的時候，幾乎每個家庭都有一本。

本書語言精練，風趣幽默，對美國人的人生觀和價值觀產生深遠的影響，被譽為「塑造美國」的88本書之一。其中，最後一章《財富之路》被公認為投資致富的經典，美國許多公司和金融機構奉如圭臬。

CONTENTS

目錄

1733年 /7

1734年 /19

1735年 /33

1736年 /45

1737年 /55

1738年 /67

1739年 /77

1740年 /87

1741年 /97

1742年 /103

1743年 /117

1744年 /127

1745年 /135

1746年 /143

1747年 /149

1748年 /157

1749年 /173

1750年 /187

1751年 /195

1752年 /205

1753年 /217

1754年 /223

1755年 /231

1756年 /237

1757年 /243

1758年 /255

1733年

愚蠢的人才會讓自己的醫生成為自己的財產繼承人。

He's a Fool that makes his Doctor his Heir.

敬愛的讀者：

在此，我想我也許可以先做出以下的聲明：我寫作曆書沒有其他的目的，純粹只是為了公眾利益，順便獲得人們對我的認同；但是其實我這樣說不算真誠，再加上現在的人們太聰明了，很難被騙到（即使是很高明的騙術），所以不真誠的話也很難站得住腳。整件事情的來龍去脈應該是：我是一個十分貧窮的人，而我的妻子，一個好女人，我經常說她過於驕傲自負。她說她無法忍受我整天只是盯著星星看，其他什麼事情都不做，她卻要忙著紡紗；她曾經不止一次地威脅我，如果我再不用那些書和咔咔作響的夾子（這就是她對我那些觀測儀器的稱呼）為家庭謀取福利，她就要一把火燒光它們。此外，出版商承諾給我一筆相當可觀的利潤分成，於是我開始遵照老婆大人的意願，動手寫作曆書。

說真的，很多年以前，我要創作曆書的動機已經很強烈，但是出於對我的好友兼同窗泰坦・利茲先生（譯者注：當時出版曆書的另一人，是作者的競爭對手）的尊敬，我非常不願意做出任何傷害他利益的事情：然而，即使是這樣的阻礙（我真的不願意用這個詞語來形容），過了不久也被清除了。因為死神從來不懂得尊重人類的勞動成果，她已經準備好致命的飛鏢——這個奪人性命的魔女已經伸長她那把要人命的剪刀，那個天才一般的男人不久就會被帶走。我曾經接受他的要求，做過以下的推算：他將會死於1733年10月17日下午3點29分，具體到xxx和xxx的xxx瞬間，那個時候剛好是太陽跟水星相交的時刻。根據他自己的推算，他可以活到同年10月的26日。就是因為我們之間的這個小差異，在過去的這九年中，無論何時我們遇見彼此，都會為這個細小的推算差別爭論得面紅耳赤，但是最終，他都會傾向於我的判斷。到底我們誰算得最準確，這個答案不久將會昭告天下。因為今年以後，很多地方的讀者可能再也看不到他的表演（譯者注：意味著泰坦·利茲先生的離世），我想我自己可以承接曆書創作這項任務，我也期望可以獲得公眾的鼓勵和支持；因此，我懇求將要購買此書的讀者們可以這樣想：我們買到的不僅是一樣有用的工具，花費的錢更是對我們窮困的朋友兼僕人——理查·桑德斯所行的善舉。

理查·桑德斯

不要捨不得喝牧師遞來的酒，也不要捨不得吃麵包師給的布丁。

Never spare the Parson's wine, nor the Baker's pudding.

去別人家做客，停留的時間要短，短如冬日的白晝，以免時間一長，被人嫌惡，反遭驅趕。

Visits should be short, like a winters day, lest you're too troublesom hasten away.

家裡沒有女人和煙火，就如同身體缺了靈魂和精神。

A house without woman & Fire-light, is like a body without soul or sprite.

守護在國王身邊的人跟養熊的人一樣，整天都提心吊膽。（譯者注：寓意為伴君如伴虎，稍有不慎，小命不保）

Kings & Bears often worry their keepers.

錢包輕癟，內心沉重。

Light purse, heavy heart.

愚蠢的人才會讓自己的醫生成為自己的財產繼承人。

He's a Fool that makes his Doctor his Heir.

沒有房子（和暖爐），娶了妻子沒處放。

Ne'er take a wife till thou hast a house (& a fire) to put her in.

他走了，除了沒有跟自己的債主們道別（交代），其他倒是什麼都沒忘。

He's gone, and forgot nothing but to say Farewel—to his creditors.

愛得深沉，打得也狠。（譯者注：愛之深，責之切）

Love well, whip well.

就讓我最尊敬的朋友J.G.接受我為他寫的這首寒詩吧！即：聰穎博學，又惹人嫉妒的青春，就按照你最初的樣子走下去吧，這樣一來，即使是你的仇敵，也會覺得猶有榮焉。

Let my respected friend J. G. accept this humble verse of me. viz. Ingenious, learned, envy'd Youth, go on as thou'st began; Even thy enemies take pride that thou'rt their countryman.

飢餓的人眼裡看不到壞的麵包。

Hunger never saw bad bread.

當心被煮熟過兩次的肉，還有和解過的宿敵。

Beware of meat twice boil'd, & an old foe reconcil'd.

口頭上的巨人，行動上的矮子。（譯者注：喜歡說大話的人，行動力都不足）

Great Talkers, little Doers.

有錢的無賴，就像肥胖的豬，從來不行好事，直到死硬倒地，像一根圓木。（譯者注：寓意為有錢的惡棍，從來沒有做過一件好事，除非死得像地上的木頭車輪停止做壞事，似乎才勉強算得上是一件好事，但是肥豬死了可以吃）

A rich rogue, is like a fat hog, who never does good til as dead as a log.

有關係卻沒有友情，有友情卻沒有權勢，有權勢卻沒有意志，有意志卻沒有效力，有效力卻沒有利潤，有利潤卻沒有道德，所有這些，全部不值一提。

Relation without friendship, friendship without power, power without will, will witho. effect, effect without profit, & profit without vertue, are not worth a farto.

吃是為了活下去，活下去卻不只是為了吃。

Eat to live, and not live to eat.

三月四月，風吹雨打，五月一到，風和日麗。

March windy, and April rainy, makes May the pleasantest month of any.

偉人給的恩賜都不是白得的。

The favour of the Great is no inheritance.

傻瓜做大餐，智者吃大餐。

Fools make feasts and wise men eat 'em.

當心年輕的醫生和年老的理髮師。

Beware of the young Doctor & the old Barber.

與其駕一匹獨眼慢馬，不如駕一匹雙目失明的好馬。

He has chang'd his one ey'd horse for a blind one.

窮人幾乎一無所有，乞丐是真的一無所有，富人則是擁有太多，但是他們卻無一人擁有滿足。

The poor have little, beggars none, the rich too much, enough not one.

讓男人三天就厭倦的事情有三件：少女、客人、雨天。

After 3 days men grow weary, of a wench, a guest, & weather rainy.

想要長壽，節制飲食。

To lengthen thy Life, lessen thy Meals.

用以檢驗真金的是烈火，用以檢驗女人的是真金，用以檢驗男人的是女人。（譯者注：寓意為真金不怕火煉，好女不拜金，好男不戀色）

The proof of gold is fire, the proof of woman, gold; the proof of man, a woman.

盛宴備好，廚師搔頭。（譯者注：寓意為準備一頓豐盛的大餐，廚師就要挖空心思、煞費苦心）

After feasts made, the maker scratches his head.

寵辱不驚的鮑伯心。

Neither Shame nor Grace yet Bob.

自從女人們不再紡紗織衣，許多的錢財就被用在喝茶花銷上。

Many estates are spent in the getting, Since women for tea forsook spinning & knitting.

與狗同臥的人，起身必帶蝨子。

He that lies down with Dogs, shall rise up with fleas.

廚房美味多，意志就薄弱。（譯者注：寓意為誘惑越大，意志越薄弱）

A fat kitchin, a lean Will.

多一些小心，多一些安全。（譯者注：寓意為小心駛得萬年船）

Distrust & caution are the parents of security.

舌頭動成影，麻煩惹上身。（譯者注：禍從口出）

Tongue double, brings trouble.

酒酣耳熱好談事，欲做決定先喝水。（譯者注：寓意為喝酒不耽誤尋求建議，但是做決策的時候需要頭腦清晰，這個時候只能喝水不能喝酒，否則會誤事）

Take counsel in wine, but resolve afterwards in water.

酒喝得急的人，錢付得慢。

He that drinks fast, pays slow.

到了狼吃狼的地步，也就到了大飢荒的時候。

Great famine when wolves eat wolves.

失去了賢妻，等於弄丟了上帝賜予的禮物。

A good Wife lost is God's gift lost.

一匹受訓的馬，一個訓人的女人，以及踐行訓誡的老師。

A taught horse, and a woman to teach, and teachers practising what they preach.

缺乏美德，正如穿衣不蔽體。

He is ill cloth'd, who is bare of Virtue.

蠢人之心嘴上放，智者之口心裡藏。

The heart of a fool is in his mouth, but the mouth of a wise man is in his heart.

人心隔肚皮，善惡難測；瓜瓤藏皮內，生熟難判。

Men & Melons are hard to know.

世間藥，多數無效；好醫生，心知肚明。

He's the best physician that knows the worthlessness of the most medicines.

絕頂的天才在自己的國家，正如黃金被埋沒在礦中——經常無用武之地。

A fine genius in his own country, is like gold in the mine.

敵人就是敵人，無大小之區分。

There is no little enemy.

他丟了自己的馬靴，但是撿回了馬刺。（譯者注：寓意為塞翁失馬，焉知非福）

He has lost his Boots but sav'd his spurs.

這個老頭生前就把所有的東西留給他的兒子：噢！真是傻瓜！就像還沒有上床睡覺就脫光自己的衣服。

The old Man has given all to his Son: O fool! to undress thyself before thou art going to bed.

乳酪和鹹肉，吃時須節制。

Cheese and salt meat, should be sparingly eat.

門和牆是傻瓜用來騙自己的障眼法。（譯者注：寓意為騙得了自己，但是防不住賊）

Doors and walls are fools' paper.

給惡棍一點甜頭嘗嘗，他反而會欺負你，但是給他一點厲害瞧瞧，他反而會巴結你。

Anoint a villain and he'll stab you, stab him & he'l anoint you.

讓你的嘴保持濕潤，腳保持乾燥。

Keep your mouth wet, feet dry.

沒有飯吃的地方，人們什麼都可以出賣。

Where bread is wanting, all's to be sold.

跟惡棍做買賣，最後只會落得名利雙失。

There is neither honour nor gain, got in dealing with a villain.

我猜，一定是傻子發了一個誓願：絕對不讓火平息下來。

The fool hath made a vow, I guess, never to let the fire have peace.

多雪的冬季，預示來年的好收成——瑞雪兆豐年。

Snowy winter, a plentiful harvest.

沒有人可以比醉漢更像傻子的。

Nothing more like a Fool, than a drunken Man.

上帝總是隨時施展神蹟。不信你瞧！老實人也可以做律師！

God works wonders now & then; Behold! A Lawyer, an honest Man!

過分放縱肉欲的人，命活不長。

He that lives carnally, won't live eternally.

清白自會辯護——清者自清。

Innocence is its own Defence.

舊時的詩人會說：時間吞沒一切。時代恆變，我們現在的時代推翻之前所有的一切。

Time eateth all things, could old Poets say; The Times are chang'd, our times drink all away.

不必擔心，節口一過，她就會清醒過來。

Never mind it, she'l be sober after the Holidays.

1734年

你想要活得輕鬆自在嗎？那就去做你應該做的，而不只是你願意做的。

Would you live with ease, do what you ought, and not what you please.

尊敬的讀者：

去年，因為你們的好心和大方的幫助——大量購買我的曆書——使得我在這個世界的情況獲得改善。現在，我的妻子擁有自己的鍋，這表示她不必再向鄰居借用，從此我們再也沒有斷過或是向別人借過可以烹煮的食材。她剛買了一雙鞋子，還買了兩套衣服替換著穿，一件新的襯裙用來保暖；我自己的部分，我買了一件二手的外套，這件外套真的很棒，因為我現在可以穿著它去城裡或是出去見人，不會感到難為情，這真是給我掙足了面子。以上所有的這些事情，使她的脾氣更平和（與之前相比），我不得不說的是，今年與去年相比，我睡得更多，也更安穩了，這一年睡得甚至比過去三年加起來睡得還要安穩。所以，請務必接受我這份發自內心的感謝，以及我對您的健康和富足的誠摯祝願。

我在上一本曆書的前言部分提前告知人們，我最親愛的老朋友，我的同窗好友，一個博聞強識、才思敏捷的人，泰坦・利茲先生的死訊。我當時的說法是：他將會死於1733年10月17日下午3點29分，具體到xxx和xxx的xxx瞬間。按照他自己的推算，他可以活到同一月份的26日，而且會在上午十一點日食出現的時刻——太陽跟水星交會的時候斷氣。在這些他「將會」或是真的會死亡的時間點，（我卻不能在我現下的寫作中明確地告訴我的讀者，哪一個時間點才是他真正會死亡的時間），因為我的行程安排隨時會被家庭瑣事打亂，所以我沒有機會在老朋友的彌留之際，即使我很想，現實也不允許我在他彌留之際送他最後一程，或是在他閉上眼睛之前，給他人生的最後一個擁抱，盡一些朋友為好友臨終送別的義務。正是因為如此，我不能很肯定地告訴我的讀者們，我的這位老友是否真的故去了；因為只有機靈的人，才可以從星象布局中讀懂自然和宇宙的因果循環鏈預示的、將要發生的事情；但眾所周知的是，那些在自然循環過程中必然發生的事件，有時候會礙於明智而理性的考量，被一種直接而特定的天意暫時擱置或延遲。然而，只是依靠研究天穹的星象，人類很難解讀出這種冥冥之中的安排。所以，（在此，我不無悲傷地說出這些話），最大的可能性就是我那個親愛的朋友已經不在人世；因為正如我確信的那樣，他的名字出現在一本1734年的曆書裡，就是在這本書裡，我被以一種非常粗俗，極其不體面，也不光彩的方式對待——在這本曆書裡，我被冠以假先知、無知者、自負的抄書者、傻瓜、說謊者等類似的稱號。

我知道利茲先生的修養甚好，所以他絕對不會使用任何卑鄙低俗的手段來對待別人，更何況他生前對我非常尊重而且喜愛。

這本手冊恐怕只是有心人的一項「發明」，這些居心叵測的人——很有可能只是想要藉由利茲先生名字的影響力和號召力來賣兩三年的曆書，賺取一些利潤。但令人氣憤的是：藉由一個紳士，一個文化人的口，他們說出極不文明的話，並且想要以此來反對他的朋友。我猜想，就算是最卑鄙、最無恥的人，哪怕是在一場酒醉的爭吵中，對於這種行為也是羞於說出口，因為說出這樣的話，對這個人的回憶將是一種不可原諒的傷害，更是對公眾的一種精神壓迫。

利茲先生不僅在他專攻的實用科學領域技藝精湛，他本人更是審慎節制的楷模，也是我最真摯的朋友和言行一致的表率。這些連同他其他的一些寶貴品格，使我們彼此之間更加要好。話雖如此，但是如果現在將我與他的預測進行對比，結論卻是：他很有可能還活著，我只會失去一個預言家的好名聲，承擔來自各方的羞辱。因為對我來說，他的生命、健康、安全才是歡樂和滿足的源頭。

敬愛的讀者，我是您的窮人朋友兼僕人。

理查・桑德斯

1733年10月30日

你想要活得輕鬆自在嗎？那就去做你應該做的，而不只是你願意做的。

Would you live with ease, do what you ought, and not what you please.

腳下打滑，好過舌頭打滑。（譯者注：寓意為摔倒比失言好）

Better slip with foot than tongue.

欲摘玫瑰怕被刺，欲娶美妻怕惹事。（譯者注：寓意為沒有玫瑰不帶刺，妻子太漂亮，容易招惹事端）

You cannot pluck roses without fear of thorns, nor enjoy a fair wife without danger of horns.

無正義，何來十足之勇氣。

Without justice, courage is weak.

吃得多，病來找；亂用藥，病難好。

Many dishes many diseases, many medicines few cures.

腐屍堆起，鷹飛來；律法健全，人聚攏。

Where carcasses are, eagles will gather, and where good laws are, much people flock thither.

熱的、利的、甜的、冷的，都會腐蝕牙齒，都會讓牙齒變成舊的。

Hot things, sharp things, sweet things, cold things all rot the teeth, and make them look like old things.

一味指責和一味讚美都是愚蠢之舉。

Blame-all and Praise-all are two blockheads.

飲酒有量，進食有度，聲色有限，懶散有數，牢牢記住，病痛找你無門路。

Be temperate in wine, in eating, girls, & sloth; or the Gout will seize you and plague you both.

無法吃苦的人，無法享福。（譯者注：吃得苦中苦，方為人上人）

No man e'er was glorious, who was not laborious.

掩飾過錯者，內心煎熬；知錯立改者，痛苦減半。

What pains our Justice takes his faults to hide, with half that pains sure he might cure 'em quite.

成功的時候要謙虛——在春風得意的時候，必須戒驕戒躁。

In success be moderate.

落魄理查的這句話，請你務必牢記：因為生氣開始的，都會以恥辱收場。

Take this remark from Richard poor and lame, whate'er's begun in anger ends in shame.

有些食物味道好，營養也好。

What one relishes, nourishes.

蠢人多做傻事。

Fools multiply folly.

美好和愚蠢向來都是好朋友。

Beauty & folly are old companions.

收穫有望，痛苦減半。

Hope of gain lessens pain.

勤勞面前，事事容易；懶惰跟前，困難重重。

All things are easy to Industry, all things difficult to Sloth.

騎馬要穩坐馬背，緊貼馬腹；馭人要鬆弛有度，收放自如。

If you ride a Horse, sit close and tight; If you ride a Man, sit easy and light.

新發現的真理是真理，已經存在的錯誤還是錯誤，但是傻子卻難以明白其中任何一點。

A new truth is a truth, an old error is an error, Tho' Clodpate wont allow either.

不要妄想只用一條獵犬就可以捕到兩隻野兔。

Don't think to hunt two hares with one dog.

占星師說，五月是尋歡作樂的季節。（譯者注：寓意為春日萬物復甦，是動物交配的季節）

Astrologers say, this is a good Day, to make Love in May.

給別人帶來歡樂的人也會收穫歡樂。

Who pleasure gives, shall joy receive.

有病不能拖，晚了沒得救；病癒如太快，好了也憂心。

Be not sick too late, nor well too soon.

只要有無愛的婚姻，就會有無關婚姻的愛來插足。

Where there's Marriage without Love, there will be Love without Marriage.

律師、牧師、山雀鳥蛋，多的是沒有孵出來的半吊子。

Lawyers, Preachers, and Tomtits Eggs, there are more of them hatch'd than come to perfection.

既不要糊塗，也不要精明，但是要有智慧。

Be neither silly, nor cunning, but wise.

如果開始示弱，就會連堡壘和處女都難以再堅持下去。

Neither a Fortress nor a Maidenhead will hold out long after they begin to parly.

小傑克，種得少，收得少。（譯者注：寓意為努力跟收穫成正比——一分耕耘，一分收穫）

Jack Little sow'd little, & little he'll reap.

節省下來的什麼都便宜，浪費掉的什麼都昂貴。（譯者注：得不到的永遠在騷動）

All things are cheap to the saving, dear to the wasteful.

勸人須談利益，勿擺道理。

Would you persuade, speak of Interest, not of Reason.

有人因為要學習的東西過多而發瘋，有人卻因為學習有助成長的東西而癲狂。

Some men grow mad by studying much to know, but who grows mad by studying good to grow.

樂即是悲，福禍相依總不長。

Happy's the Woing, that's not long a doing.

不要以技能好壞來評定一個人的價值，而是要注重他擁有的品格。

Don't value a man for the Quality he is of, but for the Qualities he possesses.

戰馬布西發拉斯擁有的名望如其主人亞歷山大擁有的名聲一般，永世長存。（譯者注：寓意為一人得道，雞犬升天）

Bucephalus the Horse of Alexander hath as lasting fame as his Master.

冷風吹，雨雪至。不久君便知，眾人亦明瞭。（如果不信）還有光陰流替，證據鑿鑿。

Rain or Snow, to Chili go, you'll find it so, for ought we know. Time will show.

與世界上最有名氣的人一樣，許多籍籍無名的人也有同樣偉大的靈魂。

There have been as great Souls unknown to fame as any of the most famous.

善待自己的朋友，你可以留住他；善待你的敵人，你可以獲得他（的心）。

Do good to thy Friend to keep him, to thy enemy to gain him.

好人難得焦慮，壞人從不安心。

A good Man is seldom uneasy, an ill one never easie.

教你的孩子學會管住舌頭，他很快就可以學會說話。

Teach your child to hold his tongue, he'l learn fast enough to speak.

不能服從命令的人，也不懂得發號施令。

He that cannot obey, cannot command.

暴君不如白丁。白丁重如泰山，暴君輕若鴻毛。

An innocent Plowman is more worthy than a vicious Prince.

山姆教派（譯者注：其意疑同「山姆大叔」，暗指美國）就像切達起司，由一二十個教區的牛奶製成。

Sam's Religion is like a Chedder Cheese, 'tis made of the milk of one & twenty Parishes.

妻子亡故會傷心，客人有難會擔憂，男人如此，終須前行，另覓開頭，兼養身心。妻子於此，非是良妻。

Grief for a dead Wife, & a troublesome Guest, continues to the threshold, and there is at rest; But I mean such wives as are none of the best.

如果說魅力全是廢話，廢話也是一種魅力。

As Charms are nonsence, Nonsence is a Charm.

今天的一枚蛋，好過明天生蛋的雞。

An Egg to day is better than a Hen to-morrow.

喝水吧，把錢放進口袋裡，至於口乾肚痛，就把它們留給大「潘趣碗」（譯者注：指喝酒的碗）吧！

Drink Water, Put the Money in your Pocket, and leave the Dry-bellyach in the Punchbowl.

富人不必節儉過生活，節儉過生活的人無須富裕。

He that is rich need not live sparingly, and he that can live sparingly need not be rich.

若要尋敵報仇，要先管好自己。

If you wou'd be reveng'd of your enemy, govern your self

邪惡的勇士會（在關鍵時刻）背棄無辜的懦夫。

A wicked Hero will turn his back to an innocent coward.

法律如蛛網捕蠅，小個頭插翅難飛，大塊頭逍遙法外。

Laws like to Cobwebs catch small Flies, Great ones break thro' before your eyes.

真奇怪，依靠矇騙過日子的人卻很難欺騙自己。

Strange, that he who lives by Shifts, can seldom shift himself.

痛處常被碰，痛上加痛；傲慢總受辱，辱外添辱。

As sore places meet most rubs, proud folks meet most affronts.

執法者應該循法而治，民眾應該服從執法者管理。（執法者應該服從法律，民眾應該服從執法者）

The magistrate should obey the Laws, the People should obey the magistrate.

天氣晴好，雨衣要帶。（譯者注：寓意為未雨綢繆，防患未然）

When 'tis fair be sure take your Great coat with you.

不是人們擁有財富，而是財富控制人們。

He does not possess Wealth, it possesses him.

特殊情況，法不必守。我知道有些律師正是以此藉口來辦案。

Necessity has no Law; I know some Attorneys of the name.

洋蔥的威力真大，惹得寡婦抹眼淚，嗆得繼承人掩面哭。

Onions can make ev'n Heirs and Widows weep.

貪婪與幸福未曾相見，何談熟悉。

Avarice and Happiness never saw each other, how then shou'd they become acquainted.

荷蘭人最謹慎，他們奉行的節儉的座右銘是：節省手裡的每一分錢。

The thrifty maxim of the wary Dutch, is to save all the Money they can touch.

人們等著運氣找上門，卻不知道晚餐在哪裡。

He that waits upon Fortune, is never sure of a Dinner.

一個有學識的笨蛋比一個無知的笨蛋更蠢笨。

A learned blockhead is a greater blockhead than an ignorant one.

任何時候，只要你願意，你可以給兒子娶妻，但是只有你能力足夠的時候，才可以把女兒嫁出去。

Marry your Son when you will, but your Daughter when you can.

以下是「答去年十二月詩文」的內容，由我的夫人——布莉姬・桑德斯太太創作。

因為喝酒的緣故，他疏於照看自己的生意，每天晚上都在酒館待到夜深，每天起床已經日上三竿，從來不關心過問自己正在嗷嗷待哺的家人，仁慈的上帝才會盡力拯救他。

但是，他可憐的妻子是因為他才會遭此禍事啊！

By Mrs. Bridget Saunders, my Dutchess, in Answer to the December Verses of last Year.

He that for sake of Drink neglects his Trade, and spends each Night in Taverns till 'tis late, and rises when the Sun is four hours high, and ne'er regards his starving Family; God in his Mercy may do much to save him.

But, woe to the poor Wife, whose Lot it is to have him.

世間事就是這麼諷刺：一無所知的人可能偶然之間成為先知，絕頂聰明的人卻碰巧錯失良機。

He that knows nothing of it, may by chance be a Prophet; while the wisest that is may happen to miss.

主與客，如果想要賓主盡歡，主人先要自己內心開懷，或是至少也要表現出開懷的樣子才可以。

If you wou'd have Guests merry with your cheer, be so your self, or so at least appear.

飢荒、瘟疫、戰爭，以及數不清的罪孽仇怨，都是人類專屬；難道這些瘟疫、戰爭、飢荒還不足以鞭笞我們的罪行，非得要我們娶妻明智才可以嗎？

Famine, Plague, War, and an unnumber'd throng of Guilt-avenging Ills, to

Man belong;

Is't not enough Plagues, Wars, and Famines rise to lash our crimes, but must our Wives be wise?

讀者，再會了，願所有的幸福快樂追隨你：願新一年的樂事和財富都來找你。

Reader, farewel, all Happiness attend thee:
May each New-Year better and richer find thee.

1735年

選朋友要慢選而慎交，換朋友需三思而後行。

Be slow in chusing a Friend, slower in changing.

敬愛的讀者：

這是我的曆書第三次出現在印刷刊物上，到目前為止，我對自己收到的支持和物質方面的鼓勵非常滿意，我也有理由期待，出版商和讀者也很滿意我的曆書；因為出版商真的很慷慨，而且總是對我寬厚大方。如果我沒有抓住每個機會來表達我的感激之情，就會顯得我忘恩負義。因為拉丁語有言：跟忘恩負義的人，沒有什麼好說的。所以作為回謝，在此，我謹向各位致以最真摯的謝意。

無論宇宙中的星體合奏而成的交響樂多麼美妙，無論群星運行得多麼和諧，可以確定的是：地球上的觀星師們從未真正和諧共處；而是在不斷對著彼此咆哮，就像第一次見面或是從來沒有見過面的野狗一樣，對著彼此，狂吠不止，抑或像是有些丈夫對自己的妻子那樣，習慣性地咆哮不休。我卻堅定地維持自己內心的平靜，從來不去得罪和冒犯別人。我一直努力堅守這樣的處事方式：儘管如此，我還是受到來自已逝的泰坦・利茲先生的惡言相待，（泰坦・利茲先生生前從來沒有使用那樣的語言來侮辱我！）我是說，我收到的是來自泰坦・利茲先生鬼魂的言語謾罵，這個「他」假裝還活著，然後藉由曆書來詆毀我的預測，想要將我置於死地。但我還是想要說，即使我很有耐心地接受「他」對我所做的一切，心裡還是憤怒難平。然而，不管他裝作什麼，毫無疑問的，他已經長埋地下，是一個死人。

我之所以會這樣說，首先是因為星辰幾乎不會令人失望，即使有例外，也只有面對智者的時候才會出現，正如拉丁諺語所說：「Sapiens dominabitur astris.（譯者注：大意為「智者統率群星」）星象也剛好預示我對他的死期做出的推論。

二來，他的父親生前也和他一樣，是一名占星師，為了維護占星術的榮譽——這份他與父親共同信奉、一同維護的榮譽，他也註定要準時死去。

第三個原因是關於他的最後兩本曆書（即1734年和1735年兩本曆書），相信每位讀過這兩本書的讀者都會覺得這兩部作品實在平淡無奇，因為曆書的風格似乎與他之前發表的相去甚遠，而且表現得差強人意。

書中的智慧箴言不再顯得「有智慧」，反而顯得庸俗平淡，其中穿插的小提示也變得既枯燥又乏味。似乎只有最後一個月開頭的那幾行暗諷占星術的詩句略微還有一些趣味，但即使是這樣的幾行詩也只有死人才寫得出來，而且把它見縫插針地放進曆書裡，活人怎麼可能願意創作類似的詩歌？

但是最終，我還是要用他自己的話來讓他承認他確實已經死了，正如拉丁諺語所說：「搬起石頭砸自己的腳（ex ore suo condemnatus est）」。他在自己1734年發表的曆書序言部分說：「桑德斯又在自己的曆書裡犯了嚴重的錯誤，即：在書中，他宣稱『根據我的推算，我可以活到所謂的1733年10月26日』，這個說法顯然跟之前所說的完全不符合。」

但是如果真的像利茲所說，他可以一直活到1733年10月26日是一個沒有事實根據而「嚴重的錯誤」，如果是這樣，他實際的死期確實是早於10月26日這個時間。所以，無論他是出於什麼目的、有什麼意圖，只要他是先於這個時間死去，他現在就是一個死人，不管他要說什麼自相矛盾的話，一切已經死無對證，也毫無意義。還有，要說他是10月26日之前已經死去，最有可能的死亡時間豈不就是我之前推算出來的10月17日？

但是如果有些人死後還會到處遊蕩，四處惹是生非，或許是因為他們先天有些不足之症，除非花費一點心思，付出一點代價，將他們放到紅海裡，給他們一點甜頭嘗嘗，否則這種習性還是很難避免、很難改掉，但是他們也不應該因為這份「自由」而變得更加肆無忌憚。

我明白一個靈魂自由的占星師對受限制和被束縛是深惡痛絕的，因為同情心作祟，我對此事的言辭也就不那麼犀利。然而，如果他的鬼魂（譯者注：暗諷那些背後使壞的幽靈寫手）無法趕快學會怎樣善待自己尚在人世的朋友，就算再怎麼不情願，我也不能總是拖著遲遲不下決心來處理此事。

我是您忠誠的朋友和僕人，

理查・桑德斯

1734年10月30日

朝前看，否則你會發現自己已經落後於人。

Look before, or you'll find yourself behind.

糟糕的評論家糟蹋最好的書，差勁的評論家埋沒好書，故而上帝送來魔鬼烹煮的肉（據說是）。

Bad Commentators spoil the best of books, so God sends meat (they say) the devil Cooks.

你開口，他奉承，人若如此，話不能信。

Approve not of him who commends all you say.

依靠勤奮和努力，老鼠一張嘴，也能咬斷繩。

By diligence and patience, the mouse bit in two the cable.

哪裡禮儀多，哪裡詭計就多。（譯者注：寓意為口蜜腹劍）

Full of courtesie, full of craft.

有陋室安居，也有薄田耕種，還有稱心如意的妻子相伴，是為大富也。

A little House well fill'd, a little Field well till'd, and a little Wife well will'd, are great Riches.

老女僕帶領猿類到那裡，在那裡老蝙蝠被變成猿類。

Old Maids lead Apes there, where the old Batchelors are turn'd to Apes.

有人態度善變如天氣，有人則不然。

Some are weatherwise, some are otherwise.

向智者敬酒的人更有智慧。——威爾斯諺語

Dyrro lynn y ddoeth e fydd ddoethach.

窮人奔波勞累才能吃飽，富人閒庭信步只為多吃。

The poor man must walk to get meat for his stomach, the rich man to get a stomach to his meat.

跑到遠處結婚的人，不是去騙別人就是被別人騙。

He that goes far to marry, will either deceive or be deceived.

眼睛裡面容不下沙子，就像神父面前，講不了笑話。

Eyes and Priests bear no Jests.

愚者之家，古已有之。

The Family of Fools is ancient.

要買必需品，則無討價處。（譯者注：要買必需品，就不要想著討價還價）

Necessity never made a good bargain.

若有一身傲骨者在前領路，卑微善乞者只能永隨其後。

If Pride leads the Van, Beggary brings up the Rear.

聰明人，何其多，有腦無用，饑腸轆轆。

There's many witty men whose brains can't fill their bellies.

重大的問題需要深思熟慮地回答。

Weighty Questions ask for deliberate Answers.

選朋友要慢選而慎交，換朋友需三思而後行。

Be slow in chusing a Friend, slower in changing.

痛苦傷身體，享樂費腦筋。

Pain wastes the Body, Pleasures the Understanding.

狡詐者盜走馬匹，智慧者只看不理。（譯者注：因為馬對陌生人——這裡特指盜馬者有攻擊性）

The cunning man steals a horse, the wise man lets him alone.

偉大的人，若肯謙恭，則得人雙倍敬重。

Humility makes great men twice honourable.

揚帆起航的船和十月懷胎的孕婦，是這個世界上公認最美好的兩樣事物。

A Ship under sail and a big-bellied Woman, are the handsomest two things that can be seen common.

看好店鋪，用心經營，必能致富。

Keep thy shop, & thy shop will keep thee.

國王的乳酪在削皮準備（譯者注：乳酪需要削掉發酵過頭的一部分）的過程中就浪費掉一半，但是沒關係，因為羊毛出在羊身上，所有的乳酪都是從老百姓那裡來的。（譯者注：隱含意思為國王只顧自己享受，哪會管老百姓死活）

The King's cheese is half wasted in parings: But no matter, 'tis made of the people's milk.

贈人之物，光彩奪目；私收之物，暗淡無華。

What's given shines, what's receiv'd is rusty.

懶散和沉默（有時候）是傻瓜的美德。

Sloth and Silence are a Fool's Virtues.

我見過的人之中，傻瓜和智者的數量不分伯仲。

Of learned Fools I have seen ten times ten, of unlearned wise men I have seen a hundred.

如果要三個人都可以守住秘密，除非其中兩個人死掉。（剩下一個人說的話也就死無對證了）

Three may keep a Secret, if two of them are dead.

以下是人類欲望心理的寫照（譯者加）：貧窮的時候想要一些東西，奢侈的時候想要很多東西，貪婪的時候什麼都想要。

Poverty wants some things, Luxury many things, Avarice all things.

謊言單腿顫立，真理雙腿穩健。

A Lie stands on one leg, Truth on two.

張口說報復之言不算什麼（有時候逞口舌之快，說一些報復人的話不算什麼），但是說出來的話可能招來報復。

There's small Revenge in Words, but Words may be greatly revenged.

詩人說：「偉大的智者們跳得高，頭也經常被撞到。」

Great wits jump (says the Poet) and hit his Head against the Post.

假裝擁有自己本來不具備的品格，這樣的人何其可笑！（譯者注：寓意類似東施效顰）

A man is never so ridiculous by those Qualities that are his own as by those that he affects to have.

因己之故，束己之腹。（譯者注：寓意為出於對自己好的目的，要學會適當克制自己）

Deny Self for Self's sake.

公眾場合節食禁酒，一人獨處卻大吃大喝。

Tim moderate fare and abstinence much prizes, in publick, but in private gormandizes.

自從愚蠢的行為變為可以博人一笑的樂舉，蠢才就有了改頭換面的可能。

Ever since Follies have pleas'd, Fools have been able to divert.

寧願自己多受傷，絕不傷害一個人。

It is better to take many Injuries than to give one.

機會是最會誘惑人的老鴇。

Opportunity is the great Bawd.

早睡覺，早起床，四肢康健，頭腦靈光，生活富足。

Early to bed and early to rise, makes a man healthy, wealthy and wise.

對上謙恭顯本分，平輩謙恭為禮貌，對下謙恭真貴族。

To be humble to Superiors is Duty, to Equals Courtesy, to Inferiors Nobleness.

看，演說家來啦！他口若懸河，言辭如流水，滔滔不絕，但是說出來的道理乏善可陳，只有一滴水的「量」。

Here comes the Orator! With his Flood of Words, and his Drop of Reason.

人年輕，心遲暮，遲早步入晚年路。（譯者注：心態老舊的年輕人，差不多也就是年紀尚輕的老人）

An old young man, will be a young old man.

不管你說什麼，薩爾都會笑。為什麼？因為她有一口好牙！（譯者注：薩爾並非笑你說的事情，而是為了在回應的同時，炫耀她的好牙齒）

Sal laughs at every thing you say. Why? Because she has fine Teeth.

無論什麼，只要是大多數人追捧的，總是有人不屑一顧，還會跑來唱反調。他們這樣做，似乎就顯得更聰明一些。

If what most men admire, they would despise, 'Twould look as if mankind were growing wise.

太陽從未抱怨自己的付出，也從未因此而要求回報。

The Sun never repents of the good he does, nor does he ever demand a recompence.

有人讓你失望，你是否因此而生氣？記住，你不能只靠自己一個人孤軍奮戰，你必須與其他人合作。

Are you angry that others disappoint you? Remember you cannot depend upon yourself.

一次改錯等於兩次挑錯，但是一次挑錯勝過兩次犯錯。

One Mend-fault is worth two Findfaults, but one Find-fault is better than two Makefaults.

讀者，我在此祝你身體健康，財源滾滾，生活幸福。願仁慈的上帝保佑你一年到頭事業順遂。

Reader, I wish thee Health, Wealth, Happiness, and may kind Heaven thy Year's Industry bless.

1736年

財富屬於會享受它的人，而不是只會擁有它的人。

Wealth is not his that has it, but his that enjoys it.

親愛的讀者們：

你們好心地接受我之前的創作成果，這給了我極大的鼓勵，也鞭策我繼續執筆寫作。然而，你們對我的青睞，一方面是對我的作品的高度認同，另一方面也讓我遭受一些人的嫉妒，還使得另一些人因此對我心懷怨恨。

我曾經因為準確地預言某個人的去世時間而聲名遠揚，儘管如此，那些居心叵測的人卻想盡辦法要用最有效的方法讓我一夜之間身敗名裂，他們宣稱我這個人根本不存在。

簡言之，用他們的話來說就是：「從來沒有我這麼一號人物」。他們到全國各地散播這個謠言，甚至於有幾次還有不認識我的人，當著我的面談論這個謠言。這種無理剝奪我本來就有的存在權，擅自向公眾宣稱我非實體存在的野蠻行徑，哪裡算得上文明之舉，簡直就是喪心病狂！

但是，只要我知道自己還可以走動、吃喝、睡覺，毫無疑問，我還是一個活生生的人，不管他們怎麼散播謠言、混淆視聽。整個世界也可以確定我是一個活生生的人；因為如果這個世界沒有我這樣一個人存在，這幾年我怎麼可能透過寫書的方式，出現在公眾的視野裡？

我的敵人們總是喜歡把我創作的功勞推給印刷商，但是我的印刷商好像不願意照顧我的「孩子」（譯者注：喻指曆書），就跟我不願意失去曆書作家的名聲，是一樣的道理。所以，為了證明他的無辜，順便也維護我自己的榮譽，我在此鄭重地做出公開聲明：我以前創作的以及我現在創作的所有作品，皆是出自我個人之手，從未假借任何男士或女士、任何個人或團體的力量。我希望各位有識之士可以慧耳辨音，相信我說的話。對我此舉還是不滿足的人，我只能說他們只是一些不講理的人。

以下是我今年的成果，仁慈的讀者，它正在靜待您的翻閱和審查，如果有過失之處，請多多海涵。它將盡其所能地為您服務，供您品鑑使用，如果有幸可以取悅它的主人——讀者您，我——窮理查・桑德斯，辛勞一年也可以感到心滿意足了。

理查・桑德斯

真正的小丑做事粗俗滑稽，田間勞作的老實人顯然不是。

He is no clown that drives the plow, but he that doth clownish things.

懂得讓自己的支出少於收入的人，擁有點金石。

If you know how to spend less than you get, you have the Philosophers-Stone.

好會計善於為別人理財。

The good Paymaster is Lord of another man's Purse.

魚放三天就會臭不可聞，客人留住三天就要遭人嫌棄。

Fish & Visitors stink in 3 days.

除非你是雷神之子，否則誰家的親戚裡沒有一些傻子、妓女、乞丐。

He that has neither fools, whores nor beggars among his kindred, is the son of a thunder-gust.

勤奮是好運之母。

Diligence is the Mother of Good-Luck.

依靠希望活著的人，死去就像放屁，毫無價值可言。

He that lives upon Hope, dies farting.

不去做自己從未瞭解的事情。

Do not do that which you would not have known.

不要向別人誇讚自己的蘋果酒、馬匹，或是跟你同榻而眠的人。

Never praise your Cyder, Horse, or Bedfellow.

財富屬於會享受它的人，而不是只會擁有它的人。

Wealth is not his that has it, but his that enjoys it.

知曉現在發生的事情很容易，知曉未來發生的事情很困難。（看當下事容易，觀未來事困難）

'Tis easy to see, hard to foresee.

任何眾人見怪不怪的事情，到了謹慎的人口中也會成為私密的事情。

In a discreet man's mouth, a publick thing is private.

你的女僕必須忠誠、強壯、質樸。

Let thy maidservant be faithful, strong, and homely.

亞麻不能靠近火苗，年輕人不能沾染賭博。

Keep flax from fire, youth from gaming.

斤斤計較的人，沒有朋友也沒有親戚。（朋友和親戚之間不要過於斤斤計較）

Bargaining has neither friends nor relations.

無故仰慕即是無知（之女）。

Admiration is the Daughter of Ignorance.

老酒鬼總是比老醫生多。

There's more old Drunkards than old Doctors.

給自己的臉塗脂抹粉來偽裝自己的人總是擔心有一天露出馬腳，被別人發現。

She that paints her Face, thinks of her Tail.

這就是真「勇氣」的寫照：趁獅子不在家鳩佔鵲巢，在老鼠面前只能落荒而逃。

Here comes Courage! That seiz'd the lion absent, and run away from the present mouse.

男人娶妻須當心，謹防喜服換綠帽。

He that takes a wife, takes care.

非禮勿視他人信，非禮勿碰（竊）他人財，非禮勿探他人事。

Nor Eye in a letter, nor Hand in a purse, nor Ear in the secret of another.

花錢分分計較的人，不僅可以養活自己，也可以供養別人。

He that buys by the penny, maintains not only himself, but other people.

有耐心，就可以擁有自己想要的一切。

He that can have Patience, can have what he will.

現在，我有了牛和羊，每個人都來祝我明天旺。

Now I've a sheep and a cow, everybody bids me good morrow.

上帝幫助自我幫助的人——天助自助者。

God helps them that help themselves.

為什麼盲人的老婆還要整天塗脂抹粉？（打扮給誰看？）

Why does the blind man's wife paint herself?

螞蟻從來不開口說教，但牠是最好的老師。（譯者注：因為牠總是以行動來身教，身教勝於言傳）

None preaches better than the ant, and she says nothing.

缺席的人一定有過錯，出席的人一定有理由。

The absent are never without fault, nor the present without excuse.

如果風透過洞口吹到你身上，就要堅定自己的意志，看顧好自己的靈魂，不要動搖。

If wind blows on you thro' a hole, make your will and take care of your soul.

一個爛蘋果「帶壞了」其他蘋果。（譯者注：一粒老鼠屎，壞了一鍋粥）

The rotten Apple spoils his Companion.

出賣別人對自己的信任，這樣的人將會失去朋友，變得窮困潦倒。

He that sells upon trust, loses many friends, and always wants money.

如果自家用的是玻璃窗，就不要向左鄰右舍扔石頭。（譯者注：謹防別人以其人之道還治其人之身）

Don't throw stones at your neighbour's, if your own windows are glass.

豬肥胖則好，人德高才妙。

The excellency of hogs is fatness, of men virtue.

家有好丈夫，年年收成好；家有省錢夫，娶妻也賢慧。

Good wives and good plantations are made by good husbands.

起疹子的是自己，怪不了別人。

Pox take you, is no curse to some people.

權力的光只照到理性的背。（權力面前，理性無光）

Force shines upon Reason's Back.

愛人、行人、詩人，自掏腰包也要訴說心聲。

Lovers, Travellers, and Poets, will give money to be heard.

多說多錯——話說得多的人，被誤解的時候也多。

He that speaks much, is much mistaken.

債主的記性總是比欠債人好。（譯者注：放債的總是比欠債的更可以記得借債的數額）

Creditors have better memories than debtors.

男人除非被別人戴了綠帽，否則必須先警告再動手。

Forwarn'd, forearm'd, unless in the case of Cuckolds, who are often forearm'd before warn'd.

男人最容易因為三樣東西而被騙：一是馬匹，二是假髮，三是嬌妻。

Three things are men most liable to be cheated in, a Horse, a Wig, and a Wife.

生活富足安逸者，學問修養也極好。

He that lives well, is learned enough.

貧困、詩歌、新頭銜，都是讓人可笑的源頭。

Poverty, Poetry, and new Titles of Honour, make Men ridiculous.

到處撒荊棘刺的人，走路最好不要光著腳。

He that scatters Thorns, let him not go barefoot.

只有被自己信任的人欺騙，才算是真正地被騙。

There's none deceived but he that trusts.

老天治病救人，醫生收取費用。

God heals, and the Doctor takes the Fees.

你的欲望之口如果打開，再多的東西也不夠填。

If you desire many things, many things will seem but a few.

瑪麗的嘴沒有花過她一毛錢，因為她從來不開口付帳，總是等著花別人的錢。

Mary's mouth costs her nothing, for she never opens it but at others expence.

簽字之前先接納，付款之前先簽字。

Receive before you write, but write before you pay.

我很少看見有人餓死，卻經常看到有人撐死。（不誇張地說，撐死的人有十萬之多）

I saw few die of Hunger, of Eating 100,000.

美國的女孩們，是誰讓你們的牙齒變壞的？答案是：熱湯和冷凍蘋果。

Maids of America, who gave you bad teeth?

Answer: Hot Soupings & frozen Apples.

趁早嫁掉你的女兒，及時吃掉新鮮的魚。

Marry your Daughter and eat fresh Fish betimes.

受到老天保佑的人，他的狗也可以生出小豬仔。（譯者注：一人得道，雞犬升天）

If God blesses a Man, his Bitch brings forth Pigs.

這樣的人才會活得平靜自在：絕不坦言自己所知的一切，絕不論斷自己所見的一切。

He that would live in peace & at ease, must not speak all he knows, nor judge all he sees.

1737年

經歷失敗與挫折，就會變得更謙遜明智。

After crosses and losses men grow humbler & wiser.

殷勤而善良的讀者：

這是我第五次出現在讀者面前，用手中的筆，我將為正直的同胞們描繪出未來一年即將發生、有可能發生，以及可能不會發生的事情。因此，我收到人們對我的普遍讚譽，這更令我滿心歡喜。

確實，我們透過觀測星象做出大量的推測，其中難免會出現少數失誤。原因是，即使觀測技術本身沒有任何缺陷，但是所有人都知道，只要有一個小失誤，只要計算中用錯一個小數值，一場大錯也就在所難免。但是我們相信我們創作曆書的人，對每個月日期的計算都是精準的，我認為，這才是最實用的東西。儘管我們可能會在曆書的其他地方犯一些小錯，但是我想這些錯誤都是無傷大雅的。

至於天氣，我如果採用我的「兄弟」J——n有時候會使用的方式，告知你，我的讀者，新英格蘭或是這裡將會降雪，這裡或是南卡羅萊納州將會降雨，北方寒冷，南方暖和，諸如此類的天氣預測，就算是出錯了，也不太可能被人發現。

但是我轉念一想，覺得1000[1]英里以外是什麼天氣似乎對任何人的用處不大，於是我總是明確地為我的讀者預測他想要知道的天氣狀況。無論他身處何地，想要知道何時的天氣。我們只希望預測的天氣在時間方面的

1. 1英里=1609.344公尺。

誤差前後不會超過一兩天，這樣就是最好的津貼回報（最好的結果）。

但是如果天氣沒有像預測得那樣變化，請把過錯歸咎到我的印刷商身上，因為有可能是他為了多放自己幾天假，隨意地刪除或是顛倒某些日期或是天氣資訊。因為不管我強調多少次，人們還是習慣性地將曆書的成功多半歸功於他，所以我覺得，曆書內容如果有錯誤，他也應該承擔一些責任，才會顯得合情合理吧？

迄今為止，人們對我的仁慈以及好心的鼓勵，我一直銘記在心，從來不敢忘記，所以在這裡，我要表達自己誠摯的謝意。

但是如果慷慨大方的讀者買了我的曆書，並且瞭解到他買書的這筆錢是如何幫助到我，讓我可以點得起舒適的爐火暖身，買得起做飯用的鐵鍋，喝得起滿滿一杯的咖啡，還讓我——一個窮困潦倒的男人和我的妻子——一個正直善良、上了年紀的好女人滿心喜悅，即使這本曆書裡有一半的書頁是空白的，相信他也不會覺得自己把錢花在錯誤的地方。

您的朋友和僕人

理查・桑德斯

給想要致富者的致富要訣

有錢唯一的好處是可以花錢。

只要你是一個精明誠實的人，就算你一年只賺6英鎊，這筆錢也可以當作100英鎊來使用。

一天隨手花掉4便士的人，一年就可以隨便花掉6英鎊，也就相當於花掉可以當作100英鎊來使用的6英鎊。

每天隨意浪費自己時間的人，日復一日的，很容易就會糟蹋掉價值相當於100英鎊的一天時間（這項特權）。

隨意浪費價值五先令時間的人，也就相當於丟掉五先令，而且可能還是狀似精明地將這五先令丟進河裡。

一個人丟掉五先令，其實不僅是失去這個數目的錢，更是失去用這五先令發財致富的機會（只要抓住這個機會，透過自身的努力，從年輕的時候開始做起，到了年老的時候，這個人會因為最初的五先令賺到一筆絕對可觀的財富，使他可以衣食無憂），這些錢很有可能是一個人從壯年至老年所能累積下來的一筆財富，一筆絕對可以讓人生活得衣食無憂的財富。

再說，願意賒帳貸款給你的人，他開出的價格肯定會在賒給你那個本金的基礎上再加上相應的利息（這些利息是付款期以內他無法使用的錢所產生的）。所以說，向別人賒帳貸款的人，要為自己購買的東西付出應有的代價。

使用現金支付的人，可以將這筆錢另作他用：這個人買進的每件物品，他都要為使用這些物品而償付相應的利息。

那麼（親愛的讀者），請你做進一步的思考，你被引誘購買自己不需要的居家用品，或是其他多餘物品的時候，你是否願意在自己的有生之年背負因為一時的購買衝動而產生的利息，還有那份因為利息而產生的複利，更有甚者，你是否願意承擔這些物品在使用過程中因為意外損壞而需要賠付的額外開支。

但是，你買東西的時候最好還是選擇以現金支付，因為賒帳放貸的人正在等著這筆壞帳帶來5個百分點的損失。為了填補這個部分的虧缺，他會以賒帳加息的方式，讓借貸者預支錢款。這樣一來，那些賒帳買東西的人，就要為他們賒的帳承擔相應比例的預付款。

使用現金支付的人，卻省去了，或是有可能省去這筆開銷。

省下一分錢就等於得到兩便士，一天攢下一針眼，一年也有四便士。

省下的就是你的（屬於你的）。積少成多。

最尊貴的國王，即使坐在最華麗的寶座上，也還是穩坐在自己的屁股上。

The greatest monarch on the proudest throne, is oblig'd to sit upon his own arse.

凡是有出息者，皆胸懷抱負。

The Master-piece of Man, is to live to the purpose.

偷吃老頭晚餐的人，反而是對老頭做了一件好事。（譯者注：老頭不吃晚餐或是少吃晚餐是好事）

He that steals the old man's supper, do's him no wrong.

一個鄉下人在兩個律師之間，就像一條魚在兩隻貓之間。

A countryman between two Lawyers, is like a fish between two cats.

懂得停下休憩的人比只會攻城拔寨的人更偉大。

He that can take rest is greater than he that can take cities.

捨不得吃乳酪的人最健康。（吝嗇於乳酪，豐盛於健康）

The misers cheese is wholesomest.

愛情和權威都討厭被分享。

Love & lordship hate companions.

摘取桂冠的捷徑是：問心無愧地為榮譽而戰。

The nearest way to come at glory, is to do that for conscience which we do for glory.

想要買東西的人本來就有餘錢可用，只是他們自己不知道，因為他們的眼睛總是盯著A的寶馬名駒和B的美屋華宇。（譯者注：人們總是吃著碗裡的，看著鍋裡的）

There is much money given to be laught at, though the purchasers don't know it; witness A's fine horse, & B's fine house.

可以使自己保持鎮定自若的人，比學富五車，才華橫溢的人更聰慧。

He that can compose himself, is wiser than he that composes books.

可憐的迪克，吃東西的時候像一個紳士，喝醉酒的時候像一個病人。

Poor Dick, eats like a well man, and drinks like a sick.

經歷失敗與挫折，就會變得更謙遜明智。

After crosses and losses men grow humbler & wiser.

世界上有三樣東西不可藏：愛、咳嗽、菸癮。

Love, Cough, & a Smoke, can't well be hid.

行動上做得好，勝過嘴上說得天花亂墜。

Well done is better than well said.

精良的細亞麻、風姿綽約的女子、熠熠生輝的黃金，都不可藉著昏暗的燭火來挑選。

Fine linnen, girls and gold so bright, Chuse not to take by candle-light.

可憑雙足行遍天下的人，也是可以養出好馬的人。

He that can travel well afoot, keeps a good horse.

愛情盡都美好，監獄全都醜怖。

There are no ugly Loves, nor handsome Prisons.

沒有什麼可以跟一個忠誠體貼的好朋友相比。

易求無價寶，難得好知己。

No better relation than a prudent & faithful Friend.

一個旅行者應該具備的三樣東西：豬鼻一般靈敏的嗅覺、鹿腿一般得勁的腳力、驢子肩背超凡的馱載力。

A Traveller should have a hog's nose, deer's legs, and an ass's back.

人若辛勤勞作，飢餓休想進門。

At the working man's house hunger looks in, but dares not enter.

一個好律師往往是一個不好的鄰居。（水至清則無魚，人至察則無徒）

A good Lawyer, a bad Neighbour.

有三樣東西在本質上是一樣的：神父、律師、死神。死神面前，不分強弱，時候一到，必被帶走。律師面前，不分對錯，官司一完，都要收費。神父面前，紅白喜事，一經著手，都有錢賺。

Certainlie these things agree, the Priest, the Lawyer, & Death all three:

Death takes both the weak and the strong.

The lawyer takes from both right and wrong,

and the priest from living and dead has his Fee.

破得最嚴重的馬車輪叫得最大聲。（譯者注：半瓶水響叮噹）

The worst wheel of the cart makes the most noise.

不要對你的醫生或律師說假話。（譯者注：寓意為不要對醫生和律師有所隱瞞，否則最後還是自己吃虧）

Don't misinform your Doctor nor your Lawyer.

據我所見，經常被移栽的樹木生長得不會比起初就穩定扎根的樹木更繁茂；經常搬遷的家庭發展得不會比起初就安定下來的家庭更興盛。

I never saw an oft-transplanted tree, nor yet an oft-removed family, that throve so well as those that settled be.

向來只有讓信安靜躺著等郵差的份，哪有讓郵差停下來等信寫好的道理。

Let the Letter stay for the Post, and not the Post for the Letter.

一天三餐都吃好，疾病卻把你來找。

Three good meals a day is bad living.

寧願生死攸關的時候求敵人，不在活蹦亂跳的時候求朋友。

'Tis better leave for an enemy at one's death, than beg of a friend in one's life.

把自己的秘密洩漏給誰，就是把自己的自由出賣給誰。

To whom thy secret thou dost tell, to him thy freedom thou dost sell.

如果想要一個稱心如意的僕人，那就自己來當吧！

If you'd have a Servant that you like, serve your self.

同時追趕兩隻野兔的人，只會讓一隻跑了，另一隻也溜了——竹籃打水一場空。

He that pursues two Hares at once, does not catch one and lets t'other go.

如果想要覓得一個整潔的妻子，請在星期六的時候做出選擇。

If you want a neat wife, chuse her on a Saturday.

既然有時間，何苦一味等待而不採取行動。

If you have time, don't wait for time.

對一個吝嗇鬼說起他的富有，對一個女人說起她的年紀，在這兩件事情上，你都討不到半分好處——因為你既得不到吝嗇鬼的財，也得不到女人的好臉色。

Tell a miser he's rich, and a woman she's old, you'll get no money of one, nor kindness of t'other.

不要一有頭疼腦熱就去看醫生，也不要一爆發雞毛蒜皮的小吵小鬧就去請律師，更不要一口渴就去找水壺。

Don't go to the doctor with every distemper, nor to the lawyer with every quarrel, nor to the pot for every thirst.

債主們一定屬於某個神秘的教派，因為他們就像是偉大的時間觀測員，總是可以精準地設定日期和分秒。（用於計算放債所得的利息或是用於提醒什麼時候應該收款）

The Creditors are a superstitious sect, great observers of set days and times.

世界上最高尚的問題是：我可以為這個世界做些什麼？

The noblest question in the world is: What Good may I do in it?

沒有什麼可以像善良一樣受歡迎的。

Nothing so popular as GOODNESS.

1738年

過度的快樂會帶來極大的痛苦，樂極生悲；
過分的自由會成為最緊的束縛，物極必反。

Nothing brings more pain than too much pleasure;
nothing more bondage than too much liberty (or libertinism).

桑德斯太太作

親愛的讀者：

上個星期，我的丈夫去了一趟波多馬克，為的是拜訪一個之前認識的老占星師，順便看看有沒有適合的地方讓我們正式地安頓下來養老。離開之前，他留下封印好的曆書，囑咐我把它送給出版商。我的心中泛起疑竇，於是等他離開以後，我立刻把書拆開，想要看看他有沒有在書中說我的壞話，或是開我的玩笑。

果然不出我所料，他真的（我猜想他只是為了找一些話來說）一開始就在前言裡指責他的妻子布麗吉特，一會兒說她（就是我）這裡不好，一會兒又說她那裡不行……

了找一些話來說吧）

真是一個不通人情的豌豆莢！難道我偶爾犯一兩次錯，還要被你大書特書，印在書上，讓全國人民都知道！這下好了，所有人都會知道這次我自以為是，下次又大吵大嚷，我什麼時候買了新裙子，什麼時候又買了其他東西。現在，全世界都知道窮迪克（理查的別稱）的妻子最近剛迷上喝茶，隨時就要喝上一點。這真是一件大事啊！也值得他寫一首歌來傳唱！就是這樣！

沒錯，我去年是從印刷商那裡收到一點茶葉，可是那有什麼關係？難道要我把它扔掉才可以嗎？總之，我覺得這個前言沒有印刷的價值，所以我把它全部擦掉了，因為我相信讀者們中意的是更好的曆書，而不是更糟的曆書。

我翻看所有的月份，發現迪克將今年大多數的日子都標注上壞天氣的術語，因此我靈機一動，在還可以落筆的地方旁邊寫上「天氣晴好」、「空氣宜人」、「陽光明媚」等字眼，以讓良善的婦人們有機會晾曬衣物。但是如果天公不作美，不按照我的套路出牌，我至少也表達自己的好意，希望她們可以領會我的好意。

我原本計畫再對一些地方進行修改，尤其是想要修改那些我不怎麼喜歡的詩，但很不幸的是，就在剛才，我弄壞自己的眼鏡。唉，看來我只能把它們原封不動地給你們讀，以此作結。

您可愛的朋友

布麗吉特・桑德斯

這個世界上有三類忠實的朋友：與你相扶到老的妻子，陪你到老的狗兒，以及你唾手可得的現金。

There are three faithful friends: an old wife, an old dog, and ready money.

那些總是只顧自己說話（卻不會聽別人說話）的人要耳朵有什麼用？不如割掉算了。

Great talkers should be cropp'd, for they've no need of ears.

如果想要自己的鞋子耐穿，就不要在鞋裡釘釘子。

If you'd have your shoes last, put no nails in 'em.

誰可以欺騙你勝過你自我欺騙？

Who has deceiv'd thee so oft as thyself?

這個世界上還有什麼事情比庸人自擾、自尋煩惱更令人痛苦的？

Is there any thing Men take more pains about than to render themselves unhappy?

過度的快樂會帶來極大的痛苦，樂極生悲；過分的自由會成為最緊的束縛，物極必反。

Nothing brings more pain than too much pleasure; nothing more bondage than too much liberty (or libertinism).

多讀書，但是不要隨便亂讀書。

Read much, but not many Books.

對於打算短期借債的人，你可以借錢給他們，但是要他們在復活節還清債務。

He that would have a short Lent, let him borrow Money to be repaid at Easter.

跟隨學識淵博者習雅文，混跡市井百姓間說俗語。

Write with the learned, pronouncc with the vulgar.

放飛快樂吧，快樂將會跟著你，你將會快樂。

Fly Pleasures, and they'll follow you.

像松鼠一樣，牠喜歡用自己的尾巴遮住自己的背。

Squirrel-like she covers her back with her tail.

比起贏得戰爭的勝利，登上凱旋的戰車，凱撒更看重的是自己能否戰勝自己。

Caesar did not merit the triumphal Car, more than he that conquers himself.

你擁有美德嗎？擁有美德，需要得到它的風姿和美好。

Hast thou virtue? Acquire also the graces & beauties of virtue.

買進太多你不需要的東西，緊接著你就要賣掉自己的必需品。

Buy what thou hast no need of, and e'er long thou shalt sell thy necessaries.

如果你已經擁有智慧和學問，請讓睿智和謙遜再為你錦上添花吧！

If thou hast wit & learning, add to it Wisdom and Modesty.

德行越高尚的人，會比王子更快樂。

You may be more happy than Princes, if you will be more virtuous.

如果與世長辭，就只能長埋地下。如果想要生前留名，這裡有兩個建議可供參考：一是寫下值得閱讀的文字，二是留下值得被寫下的事蹟。

If you wou'd not be forgotten, as soon as you are dead and rotten, either write things worth reading, or do things worth the writing.

不要出賣道德以換取財富，也不要出賣自由來換取權力。

Sell not virtue to purchase wealth, nor Liberty to purchase power.

上天保佑君王，君王才可以長治久安。

God bless the King, and grant him long to Reign.

惡習不能帶進棺材裡。

Let thy vices die before thee.

婚前你要睜大眼睛，務必事事看清楚，婚後就要睜一隻眼閉一隻眼。（譯者注：難得糊塗，凡事不要太過苛求）

Keep your eyes wide open before marriage, half shut afterwards.

古人經常告訴我們什麼是最好的，但是我們必須立足於現實，擇其精華，選擇最適合我們的內容。

The ancients tell us what is best; but we must learn of the moderns what is fittest.

既然我管不住自己牙齒之間的舌頭，又哪裡來的本事去管其他人的舌頭？（哪裡管得了別人說什麼）

Since I cannot govern my own Tongue, tho' within my own teeth, how can I hope to govern the Tongues of others?

為蠅頭微利而向別人低聲下氣，比跟人討價還價更讓人不齒。

'Tis less discredit to abridge petty charges, than to stoop to petty Gettings.

既然你連一分鐘都把握不住，就不要輕易浪費掉一個小時。

Since thou art not sure of a Minute, throw not away an Hour.

如果你做了不應該做的事情，就要聽你不想聽的話。

If you do what you should not, you must hear what you would not.

行善舉，要及時，莫拖延；勿學聖喬治，端坐馬背上，不揮馬鞭，驅馬向前。

Defer not thy well-doing; be not like St. George, who is always on a horseback, and never rides on.

不求活過百歲，只求活得歡欣。

Wish not so much to live long, as to live well.

正如我們必須為自己的每句閒話負責，我們也必須為自己每次無理由的沉默辯解。

As we must account for every idle Word, so we must for every idle Silence.

我從未見過可以點石成金的魔法石，但是親眼見過那些搜尋點金石的人把自己擁有的金子變成石頭。

I have never seen the Philosopher's Stone that turns lead into Gold, but I have known the pursuit of it turn a Man's Gold into Lead.

絕對不能讓自己的僕人跟自己住在一起。

Never intreat a servant to dwell with thee.

時間是可以治百病的草藥。

Time is an herb that cures all Diseases.

閱讀使人充實完備，沉思使人深刻寬厚，交談使人思路明晰。

Reading makes a full Man, Meditation a profound Man, discourse a clear Man.

只要有人說好話恭維我，我就會說好話恭維他，即使那個人是我的知己摯友。

If any man flatters me, I'll flatter him again; tho' he were my best Friend.

祝一個小氣鬼長壽，這樣的祝福對他沒有什麼好處。

Wish a miser long life, and you wish him no good.

只有涵養極好的人才會懂得如何承認錯誤，或是及時承認做事的時候犯下的錯誤。

None but the well-bred man knows how to confess a fault, or acknowledge himself in an error.

要操持自己的事業，而不是讓你的事業驅使你、奴役你。

Drive thy business; let not that drive thee.

冒充一個好人跟效仿一個好人有天壤之別。

There is much difference between imitating a good man, and counterfeiting him.

小錯當前，擠眼放過；大錯既出，須記心間。（小錯輕放過，大錯記

心間）

Wink at small faults; remember thou hast great ones.

在吃上要取悅自己，在穿上要取悅別人。（飲食上，要吃得讓自己歡欣；穿著上，要穿得讓別人舒心）

Eat to please thyself, but dress to please others.

盡力發掘別人的優點，找出自己的缺點。

Search others for their virtues, thyself for thy vices.

不要捨不得喝牧師遞來的酒（譯者注：基督教裡為舉行聖餐牧師會向教徒提供葡萄酒，預示基督受難的鮮血），也不要捨不得吃麵包師給的布丁。

Never spare the Parson's wine, nor the Baker's Pudding.

每年都改掉一個惡習，最終惡人也可以改頭換面。

Each year one vicious habit rooted out, in time might make the worst Man good throughout.

1739年

耳不聞朋友惡言，嘴不說敵人壞話。

Hear no ill of a Friend, nor speak any of an Enemy.

好心的讀者：

因為您之前的慷慨之舉——支持和鼓勵，我將再次把新一年的曆書——我的第七本作品呈現到您的面前，供您閱讀。您大方地將自己的便士用來買書，進而轉進我的錢包裡的時候，您實際上正在幫助我，為我的小屋添置必需品，對此，窮迪克沒齒難忘您的這份恩情，也願意隨時為您效勞。

就像老貝斯（譯者注：疑指桑德斯的妻子，布麗吉特）緊緊盯著自己的女兒一樣，我也仔細地注視星象的變化，以便告知您，讓您瞭解它們的運行，也由此推測出它們會對您產生怎樣的影響，這可能比你做夢夢見去年的雪還要有用。

總是有一些無知的人想要知道占星師如何將天氣變化推測得這樣精確，有人甚至懷疑他們（占星師）是否借助某種古老的黑暗力量。嗚呼！這就跟尿床一樣簡單啊！舉例來說，這就像一個占星師用長筒望遠鏡觀察天空，他也許看到金牛座，或是那個形似大公牛的星座，正在自己的屋子裡不停地踏著蹄子，甩動著尾巴，伸長了脖子，張大著嘴巴，氣勢洶洶地狂奔。很自然的，占星師就可以從這些現象判斷出這頭憤怒的公牛正在一邊喘氣一邊咆哮。接下來將距離和時間考慮進去之後，占星師就可以推測出這可能預示狂風暴雷的來臨。

此時，他要是瞥見處女座轉過頭來，觀察是否有人在盯著她看，透過望遠鏡，你會看到她優雅地蹲下身來，雙手放在膝蓋上，殷切地注視前方。看到這裡，占星師立刻就會明白她這樣做代表什麼意思：對距離和時間進行計算之後，他就可以推測出來年春天會在四月有一場連綿陣雨。所以，還有什麼可以比這個更簡單、更自然的嗎？

我甚至還可以列舉出很多類似的例子，但是我覺得以上兩個已經足以說明我們占星師不是像巫師一樣，只是依靠裝神弄鬼謀生。噢，我們可以從星辰之間尋覓到多少奧秘啊！只要你可以讀懂，即使是微不足道的事情，你也可以從星空中找到答案。如果我的兄弟J——m——n想要知道他生病的馬兒應該喝什麼，是喝新下的蛋液，還是喝一點肉湯，他發現頭頂上的星星給他明確的指示：喝肉湯最好。於是，他餵馬喝下了肉湯。那麼，你認為那匹馬後來怎麼樣了？在我的下一本曆書中，你將會找到答案。

除了一本曆書應該具備的內容以外，我還在其中插入一些與道德和宗教相關的指示性內容，希望此舉不會被那些自詡為人師的人詬病。噢，態度嚴肅認真、頭腦清醒謹慎的讀者，如果您在許多嚴肅的話語中發現我偶爾寫出幾句詼諧逗趣的話，請相信我真的不是有意打擾您，也請您不必把這些玩笑話放在心上。到目前為止，在我為您準備的所有菜色中，已經有足量的硬菜（譯者注：肉菜），讓你覺得這筆錢花得很值得。有一些是智慧餐桌上剩下來的菜色，雖然是剩菜，但是如果可以好好消化一番，也可以產生滋養心智的作用。如果沒有餐前小菜來開胃（雖然除了開胃也沒有其他什麼作用），太過嬌貴的胃就不能享受這些剩菜。要是愛慕虛榮的年輕人為了找一些無聊的笑話來打發時間，而閱讀我的曆書，我相信他們多少也會做一些深刻的反省，這樣一來，他們或許也可以從中獲益。

有些人看到我曆書的年需求量達到一個非常可觀的數目，進而想像我現在一定很有錢，這樣一來，我不應該再自稱窮迪克。但事實是，我第一次出書的時候，與印刷商簽訂一份《公平協議》，協議規定印刷商可以拿走大部分的利潤。但是無論如何，我不會因此而怨恨他，就讓他多賺一些吧！我非常敬重他，也希望他的利潤跟現在比可以再多出十倍。因為我是您的——親愛的讀者，也是他摯愛的朋友。

理查・桑德斯

死神掐滅我們生命燭光的時候，空中殘存的氣息會證明我們是石蠟還是牛脂。

When Death puts out our Flame, the Snuff will tell, if we were Wax, or Tallow by the Smell.

哪怕只是價值一便士的小便宜，也要停下來想想是否可以貪。

At a great Pennyworth, pause a while.

談到自己的妻子，約翰想到了聖保羅，他（聖保羅）就是這樣一個人：已經娶妻了，卻好像沒有妻子一樣。

As to his Wife, John minds St. Paul, He's one that hath a Wife, and is as if he'd none.

想要壽命長，就要活得好，因為愚蠢和邪惡會減壽。

If thou would'st live long, live well; for Folly and Wickedness shorten Life.

說「請（古言）」不是克洛伊小姐的一件滑稽事嗎？

Prythee isn't Miss Cloe's a comical Case?

她總是把自己的尾巴借給別人，而向別人借來面子。

She lends out her Tail, and she borrows her Face.

只要你信任自己，別人就不會背叛你。

Trust thyself, and another shall not betray thee.

工作還沒有做完就提前付錢的人，他的一便士價值兩便士。

He that pays for Work before it's done, has but a pennyworth for twopence.

史學家寫的並非真實發生的事情，而是他們相信發生了的事情。

Historians relate, not so much what is done, as what they would have believed.

噢，酒館老闆！把那個欺騙人（缺斤少兩）的沽酒器砸了吧，這種小伎倆太容易讓人看穿了，因為使用它的人，不是流氓就是無賴啊！

O Maltster! Break that cheating Peck; 'Tis plain, when e'er you use it, you're a Knave in Grain.

讓你的家因為你而充滿榮光吧，不要依靠自己的家獲得光彩。

Grace thou thy House, and let not that grace thee.

不能指望笑話幫你化敵為友，但是有可能弄巧成拙，幫你化友成敵。

Thou can'st not joke an Enemy into a Friend; but thou may'st a Friend into an Enemy.

眼裡容不下一粒沙子，牧師無法容忍人們對上帝的褻瀆。

Eyes & Priests bear no Jests.

唯有自戀的人沒有情敵。

He that falls in love with himself, will have no Rivals.

給孩子上的第一課應該是服從，然後才是你想要教的東西。

Let thy Child's first Lesson be Obedience, and the second may be what thou wilt.

無所求的人有福了，因為他從來不會遭遇失望。（譯者注：知足者常樂）

Blessed is he that expects nothing, for he shall never be disappointed.

肚腹空空入睡，好過負債累累吃早餐。（寧願餓著肚子睡覺，也不要身負重債醒來）

Rather go to bed supperless, than run in debt for a Breakfast.

讓你的怨憤不滿成為秘密吧！

Let thy Discontents be Secrets.

治牙痛的一個妙方：用老醋清洗病齒，然後在陽光下曝曬半個小時至乾燥，這樣以後就不會再疼了——這是經過別人驗證的好方法。

An infallible Remedy for the Tooth-ach, viz Wash the Root of an aching Tooth, in Elder Vinegar, and let it dry half an hour in the Sun; after which it will never ach more——Probatum est.

學識淵博的人猶如肥沃的土地，地上長滿的不是糧食就是雜草。

A Man of Knowledge like a rich Soil, feeds if not a world of Corn, a world of Weeds.

現代人所謂的智者，大多是古代人眼中的傻瓜。

A modern Wit is one of David's Fools.

懺悔過後下定的決心不可當真。

No Resolution of Repenting hereafter, can be sincere.

波利奧，從來不關注內在，總是以貌取人，買書就像捕海狸，海狸只要皮毛亮，買書只看封皮好。

Pollio, who values nothing that's within, buys books as men hunt Beavers, for their Skin.

想要榮耀你的父母，就要過好自己的人生，讓他們即使泉下有知也覺得臉上有光。

Honour thy Father and Mother, i.e. Live so as to be an Honour to them tho' they are dead.

你若傷害良知，假以時日，良知向你報復。

If thou injurest Conscience, it will have its Revenge on thee.

耳不聞朋友惡言，嘴不說敵人壞話。

Hear no ill of a Friend, nor speak any of an Enemy.

還清你欠的債，就會知道屬於你的到底是什麼。

Pay what you owe, and you'll know what's your own.

對別人，不要捨不得讚美、勸告、鼓勵，因為這些都不會花你一分錢。

Be not niggardly of what costs thee nothing, as courtesy, counsel, & countenance.

孜孜不倦地求取功勞，而不是回報。

Thirst after Desert, not Reward.

當心不輕易生氣的人，因為人們生氣都有原因，而且是不會輕易消氣的。

Beware of him that is slow to anger: He is angry for something, and will not be pleased for nothing.

美德亡則自由亡——這是個人的信條，亦是國家的警言。

No longer virtuous no longer free; is a Maxim as true with regard to a private Person as a common-wealth.

正如詩人吟唱的那樣：男人死的時候，最後停止跳動的是心臟；女人死的時候，最後停止移動的是舌頭。

When Man and Woman die, as Poets sung, his Heart's the last part moves, her last, the tongue.

你知曉的、虧欠的、擁有的以及力所能及的一切，都不應該和盤托出。

Proclaim not all thou knowest, all thou owest, all thou hast, nor all thou can'st.

先人的江山歸先人，自己的財富靠自己。讓父輩和祖輩因為行善而流芳百世，讓我們也憑自己的努力贏得一世英名吧！

Let our Fathers and Grandfathers be valued for their Goodness, ourselves for our own.

只顧自己埋頭勤奮苦幹，哪需雙手合十求神拜佛。

Industry need not wish.

罪惡因為有害被禁止，並非因為被禁止才有害。責任並非因為強制而有益，而是因為有益才要強制。

Sin is not hurtful because it is forbidden, but it is forbidden because it's hurtful. Nor is a Duty beneficial because it is commanded, but it is commanded because it's beneficial.

每個人都說A機智，何故？因為寫作？非也，正好不是寫作這一科。

A ---- , they say, has Wit; for what?

For writing? -- No; For writing not.

喬治毫不費力就登上王座。啊！聽偽裝者說，我可以這麼做嗎？

George came to the Crown without striking a Blow.

Ah! quoth the Pretender, would I could do so.

愛，還要可（被）愛。

Love, and be lov'd.

懶骨頭哇！若非老天為你設定用途，祂為何給你手腳？

O Lazy-Bones! Dost thou think God would have given thee Arms and Legs, if he had not design'd thou should'st use them?

療癒詩歌的方法：七個富庶城邦為獲得死去的荷馬你爭我奪，但是荷馬活著的時候，人們卻朝乞討的荷馬扔石頭。

A Cure for Poetry: Seven wealthy Towns contend for Homer, dead, Thro' which the living Homer beg'd his Bread.

傾城之貌、舉國之力、萬貫之財實則並無大用，心術正則無敵。

Great Beauty, great strength, & great Riches, are really & truly of no great Use; a right Heart exceeds all.

1740年

不要懼怕死亡，因為我們死得越快，不朽的時間就會越長。

Fear not Death; for the sooner we die, the longer shall we be immortal.

殷勤的讀者：

也許您還記得，在我1733年出版的那本曆書裡——也是我的第一本曆書裡，我預言我親愛的朋友泰坦・利茲的死亡時間，即1733年10月17日下午3點29分。這位好人也似乎是按時去世，但是另外兩個人W.B.和A.B.還在以他的名義發表曆書，並且堅稱利茲尚在人世。直到真相大白於世，他們才不得已在自己1739年出版的曆書中「承認」利茲先生已經去世的既定事實，但還是堅稱利茲先生真正離世的時間是去年，而不是1733年。他們甚至對外宣稱，利茲先生在彌留之際將未來七年所有的預測留給他們。

哈，我的朋友們，這是多麼容易被戳破的謊言和偽裝啊！如果您當時沒有無端指責我是一個冒牌的預言家，我確實不會去注意哪怕一點這個方面的消息。但是您向我潑的這盆髒水，還是深深地傷害我，因為我如果要謀生，就要給予您反擊，以維護我的正當利益。

但是為了解決這場爭議，我有必要讓人們瞭解一個事實，儘管這可能會讓人聽起來覺得難以置信，但是確實句句屬實。內容如下所述，即：

本月四日將近午夜的時候，我坐在小書房裡寫這篇前言，但是不久我就睡著了。據我所知，我睡了一段時間，但是沒有夢見什麼。在我醒過來之後，我發現自己面前放著一封信。信的內容如下：

親愛的朋友桑德斯：

即使我已經與你分離，身處另一個世界，但是我對你的敬重從未改變，看到貪婪的曆書出版者因為嫉妒你的成功，冒用我的名字向你潑髒水，誹謗你的時候，我的心中非常不是滋味。他們甚至說，你關於我死期的預言是胡言亂語，並且假裝我1733年之後還活了很多年。

但是在此處，我需要澄清，我確實是在你預言的那個時刻離開人間，也就是在下午3點（你預言的時間點），只是有5分53秒的誤差，這個誤差在那樣的情況下是無傷大雅的，也是在被允許的範圍之內。此外，我還要澄清的是，我從未將任何關於未來七年的預測留給任何人，包括他們在內，儘管他們總是喜歡提起這個「假裝的事實」。所以結論就是，他們用我的名義出版的曆書，既不是出自你的手，也跟我沒有關係。

你也許想要知道這封信怎麼出現在你的書桌上。你必須瞭解，在所有帳目——所有塵緣結束之前，沒有靈魂可以脫離限制，獲得安息。所以，在此之前，我們可以到自己喜歡的地方遊蕩，拜訪老朋友，看看他們的近況，有時候進入他們的想像中，在他們清醒或是沉睡的情況下，都可以給他們一些有用的提示。於是，發現你睡著了，我就從你左邊的鼻孔進入你的大腦裡，並且找到可以控制你的右手和手指的神經末梢。在它們的幫助下，我借用你的手，寫下這封信，當時的你毫無意識。但是如果當時你睜開眼睛，你會看到正在奮筆疾書的手是你的，紙上的字跡卻是我的。

在這個沒有宗教信仰的時代，人們或許很難相信這個故事。但是你可以告訴他們三個預言，將來事實自然會讓他們信服。明年六月中旬，由於受到一個鄉村學校校長的蠱惑，星象學家J. J——n會公開跟羅馬教廷和解，並且把他所有的動產和不動產全部捐給教廷。接下來的9月7日，我的老朋友W. B.——會在這一天以內，連續9個小時不沾酒，保持頭腦清醒，這個舉動會嚇到他的左鄰右舍。同一時間，W. B. 和A. B. 將會視事實與常識為無物，繼續以我的名義出版另一本曆書。

自從我掙脫血肉之軀的束縛，並且驅散之前一直縈繞於眼前的迷霧之後，我可以更清楚地看進未來裡。我會跟隨我的善念，繼續幫助你，經常告知你即將發生的事情，為你的曆書更加精進做出努力。

親愛的迪克，我是你摯愛的朋友，

泰坦．利茲

以我自己而言，我堅信以上這封信確實是出自利茲之手。要是讀者對此還有疑惑，請持續關注那三個預言。但是如果三個預言都沒有實現，信與不信就在於您。

我是他卑微的朋友

理查•桑德斯

每個人皆有十足勇氣承擔別人苦痛，幫助別人脫離苦海。

To bear other People's Afflictions, every one has Courage enough, and to spare.

難怪湯姆會變胖，這個臃腫的罪人，誰叫他一輩子都在吃晚餐，除此之外，別無其他。

No wonder Tom grows fat, th' unwieldy Sinner, makes his whole Life but one continual Dinner.

空袋子，難立直。

An empty Bag cannot stand upright.

歷史的走向沒有偏差，是時代之幸，社稷之福。

Happy that nation, fortunate that age, whose history is not diverting.

何為蝴蝶？說到底也就是一隻穿著彩衣的毛毛蟲。

What is a butterfly? At best he's but a caterpiller drest.

紈絝子弟，金玉其外敗絮其內。（花花公子，金玉其表）

The gaudy Fop's his picture just.

輕信人者，易被人騙。

None are deceived but they that confide.

真敵放明槍，明槍易躲；假友射暗箭，暗箭難防。

An open Foe may prove a curse;

But a pretended friend is worse.

狼吃羊，並非常事；人食羊，卻已普通。

A wolf eats sheep but now and then, ten Thousands are devour'd by Men.

人之舌，軟而無骨；動一動，擊垮男人。

Man's tongue is soft, and bone doth lack;

Yet a stroke therewith may break a man's back.

飯到嘴邊還想肉，貪心不足失白粥。

Many a Meal is lost for want of meat.

對任何一種顯而易見的美，人們都選擇性看不見，但是對每一處瑕疵，都可以招惹嫉妒心。

To all apparent Beauties blind, each Blemish strikes an envious Mind.

窮人囊中羞澀，乞丐囊空如洗；富人腰纏萬貫，卻無人知足。

The Poor have little, Beggars none; the Rich too much, enough not one.

在這個世界上，有人身閒，有人意懶。

There are lazy Minds as well as lazy Bodies.

弄虛作假，背信棄義，皆屬笨蛋專利；足智多謀，誠意相待，皆與蠢人無關。

Tricks and Treachery are the Practice of Fools, that have not Wit enough to be honest.

傑克實在慷慨（譯者注：反諷），給別人建議，從不吝惜；別人給建議，絕不收下。

Who says Jack is not generous? He is always fond of giving, and cares not for receiving.——What? Why; Advice.

不畏艱辛的人，從無人知曉的海域航向無人踏足的土地，所見美景，盡都奇異：他會描繪出哪些更奇妙的風光？

The Man who with undaunted toils, sails unknown seas to unknown soils, with various wonders feasts his Sight: What stranger wonders does he write?

不要懼怕死亡，因為我們死得越快，不朽的時間就會越長。

Fear not Death; for the sooner we die, the longer shall we be immortal.

別人爭吵，你來插話，引火燒身，咎由自取。

Those who in quarrels interpose, must often wipe a bloody nose.

與人承諾可以帶來朋友，輕言無信將會變友為敵。

Promises may get thee Friends, but Nonperformance will turn them into Enemies.

我們可以在別人身上發現缺點，責怪他們的眼睛被迷住了；我們可以看到別人的小缺點，對自己的大缺點卻視而不見。

In other men we faults can spy, and blame the mote that dims their eye; Each little speck and blemish find; To our own stronger errors blind.

對別人說話，看著他的眼睛；聽別人說話，看著他的嘴巴。

When you speak to a man, look on his eyes; when he speaks to thee, look on his mouth.

珍啊，你為何淚流滿面？又為何垂頭喪氣？難道是你另一個丈夫過世了嗎？還是發生更丟臉的事情？你的丈夫過世以後，沒有人想要成為你的下一任丈夫嗎？

Jane, why those tears? Why droops your head? Is then your other husband dead? Or doth a worse disgrace betide? Hath no one since his death apply'd?

看到周邊所有的人，尤其是你自己。

Observe all men; thyself most.

最好跟希臘哲學家一起吃鹽，也不要纏著義大利侍臣要糖吃。

Thou hadst better eat salt with the Philosophers of Greece, than sugar with the Courtiers of Italy.

美德須上下求索，變為己用；其餘的，盡人事而聽天命。

Seek Virtue, and, of that possest, To Providence, resign the rest.

結婚對象門不當戶不對，雖是夫妻，卻像主僕。女人如果嫁給比自己地位高的男人，就相當於給自己找了一個主人。

Marry above thy match, and thou'lt get a Master.

內心害怕自己作惡的人，沒有其他事情需要懼怕。

Fear to do ill, and you need fear nought else.

嘲弄人者，與人結仇。

He makes a Foe, who makes a jest.

自視聰明的人，莊嚴肅穆的貓頭鷹也看不起你的時候，你的冷靜自持還可以維持下去嗎？

Can grave and formal pass for wise, when Men the solemn Owl despise?

有人因為只會傻乎乎捨不得花錢而被別人嘲笑，其他人卻因為花錢漫不經心，大肆鋪張而成為別人口中的笑柄，但是最大的傻瓜是那些把錢留著買後悔藥的人。

Some are justly laught at for keeping their Money foolishly, others for spending it idly: He is the greatest fool that lays it out in a purchase of repentance.

誰要是認識傻瓜，一定也認識傻瓜的手足，因為這兩兄弟之中，任何一人都會推薦另外一人。

Who knows a fool, must know his brother;
For one will recommend another.

避免不正當的收益：因為罪惡帶來的痛苦是多少金錢都償付不清的。

Avoid dishonest Gain: No price can recompence the Pangs of Vice.

受人幫助，銘記在心；幫助別人，不必掛礙。

When befriended, remember it: When you befriend, forget it.

偉大的靈魂總是與深切的憐憫之情融為一體，懦弱的暴君絕對不會感受得到。

Great souls with gen'rous pity melt; Which coward tyrants never felt.

如果你想要透過節省時間以騰出空閒時光，就要善加利用自己的每一分、每一秒。

Employ thy time well, if thou meanest to gain leisure.

拍馬屁的人從不顯荒謬，被拍的馬人卻信以為真。

A Flatterer never seems absurd: The Flatter'd always take his Word.

借錢給你的敵人，你會贏得他的心（化敵為友）；借錢給你的朋友，卻會失去這個朋友（變友為敵）。

Lend Money to an Enemy, and thou'lt gain him, to a Friend and thou'lt lose him.

不到七個基督彌撒結束，絕對不能稱讚或是批評。

Neither praise nor dispraise, till seven Christmasses be over.

1741年

欲評判別人過錯，先向內自我覺察，捫心自問。

E'er you remark another's Sin, bid your own Conscience look within.

無獸不成林。

No Wood without Bark.

享受當下，不忘過往；唯其如此，則對死亡無所畏懼，對末日亦無期待。

Enjoy the present hour, be mindful of the past; and neither fear nor wish the Approaches of the last.

能手秘訣：自己教自己學的人，師父往往是笨蛋。

Learn of the skilful: He that teaches himself, hath a fool for his master.

舌頭有節制，話說點子上；

話說太多，白費口舌；絮絮叨叨話不絕，轉眼一瞬人皆散：這也難怪，聽派伊嘮叨，誰人會愛？

Best is the Tongue that feels the rein; ——He that talks much, must talk in vain; We from the wordy Torrent fly: Who listens to the chattering Pye?

想像加圖（譯者注：疑為古羅馬政治家、哲學家）是瞭解你的。

Think Cato sees thee.

猴子吐口水，熱情好客，對最熱心的朋友，他們一樣照咬不誤。

Monkeys warm with envious spite, their most obliging FRIENDS will bite.

取笑走出門，奚落帶進門，兩個一見面，口舌惹上門。

Joke went out, and brought home his fellow, and they two began a quarrel.

心中不滿心中藏，爛在肚裡無人知；某日公之於世界，遭人白眼更煩心。

Let thy discontents be thy Secrets; ——if the world knows them, 'twill despise thee and increase them.

欲評判別人過錯，先向內自我覺察，捫心自問。

E'er you remark another's Sin, bid your own Conscience look within.

怒氣愚昧相依相偎，前腳剛走；懊悔惋惜聞風而來，後腳跟上。

Anger and Folly walk cheek-by-jole; Repentance treads on both their Heels.

提姆，你生氣地說要放棄自己的信仰，以後絕對不做相關的事，說相關的話：難道追隨魔鬼比追隨穆罕默德更好？

Turn Turk Tim, and renounce thy Faith in Words as well as Actions: Is it worse to follow Mahomet than the Devil?

表達感激，不要太過；如果過多，當心被踢。

Don't overload Gratitude; if you do, she'll kick.

隨時為自己產生的懶惰念頭感到無地自容。

Be always asham'd to catch thyself idle.

願意換另一個乳房哺乳的母親，哪裡可以找到？

Where yet was ever found the Mother, who'd change her booby for another?

二十歲的時候，人類的意志佔據統治地位；三十歲的時候，換理解力來接手；到了四十歲，辨識力成為主宰。

At 20 years of age the Will reigns; at 30 the Wit; at 40 the Judgment.

基督教導我們，對傷害要容忍；策略告訴我們，想盡方法避開傷害。

Christianity commands us to pass by Injuries; Policy, to let them pass by us.

謊言騎在債務背上——人負重債，謊話連篇。

Lying rides upon Debt's back.

沒有事情需要操心的人，就沒有事情可以讓他們費神。

They who have nothing to be troubled at, will be troubled at nothing.

丈夫眼裡，妻子毫無缺點——情人眼裡出西施，外人眼中，看得分明：（群眾的眼睛卻是雪亮的）不說出來，只是為了給你留面子。

Wife from thy Spouse each blemish hide more than from all the World beside: Let DECENCY be all thy Pride.

迪克的激情，越來越膨脹，越來越強烈；反觀他的理解力，看起來卻越來越弱。

Dick's Passions grow fat and hearty; his Understanding looks consumptive!

邪惡若不降臨，恐懼盡都虛妄。邪惡若真出現，恐懼也都無用，只是徒增痛苦。

If evils come not, then our fears are vain: And if they do, Fear but augments the pain.

如果不想讓敵人知道你的秘密，就不要把秘密告訴你的朋友。

If you would keep your Secret from an enemy, tell it not to a friend.

掠奪不是為了燔祭。

Rob not for burnt offerings.

貝絲自誇為「美女」，並且表示自己可以證明；看她怎樣做到？因為，先生啊！她的乳名就叫做「美麗」。

Bess brags she 'as Beauty, and can prove the same; as how? Why thus, Sir, 'tis her puppy's name.

懶漢，懶漢，快起床，生命時光莫荒廢；
有朝一日身入土，昏天暗地睡個夠。

Up, Sluggard, and waste not life; in the grave will be sleeping enough.

一份工作做得好相當於做兩份工作。（做得好，即可事半功倍）

Well done, is twice done.

請說清楚，迷惑／霧先生！你完全是用希臘語解釋英語嘛！

Clearly spoken, Mr. Fog! You explain English by Greek.

弗爾米奧，以同樣的心為自己的罪行哀悼，即將分離的朋友也還是朋友。請相信，弗爾米奧，不到重逢之時，喜樂不會降臨。

Formio bewails his Sins with the same heart, as Friends do Friends when they're about to part. Believe it, Formio, will not entertain, one chearful Thought till they do meet again.

榮譽加身，舉止改變——得意忘形。

Honours change Manners.

吃著過期的乳酪，傑克說，像辛普森，我殺死的人有千萬個；我可以作證，羅傑說，確實如此，而且你們使用的還是同樣的武器。

Jack eating rotten cheese, did say, like Sampson I my thousands slay; I vow, quoth Roger, so you do, and with the self-same weapon too.

跟傻瓜相比，聰明人更令人生厭。

There are no fools so troublesome as those that have wit.

如果錯誤只是在一方身上，爭吵就不會無休無止。

Quarrels never could last long, if on one side only lay the wrong.

勿叫玩樂誘惑，勿讓利益吸引，勿被野心腐蝕，莫讓先例誤導，莫因勸說動搖，只有這樣，才不會犯下明知不可犯的錯，做出不可為的惡；也只有這樣，才可以生活喜樂：因為良知光明，每天都是聖誕節。

Let no Pleasure tempt thee, no Profit allure thee, no Ambition corrupt thee, no Example sway thee, no persuasion move thee, to do any thing which thou knowest to be Evil; So shalt thou always live jollily: for a good Conscience is a continual Christmass.

1742年

你明天有要做的事情嗎？今天就開始著手進行吧！

Have you somewhat to do tomorrow? Do it today.

謙恭的讀者：

以曆書作者的身分盡心為您效力，今年已經是第九年了。至今為止，我收到的所有鼓勵和支持，在很大程度上都是源自讀者的慈善之心，我因為第一次公開露面的時候就坦言自己的窮困境遇，這也激起讀者您的同情心，並且使我收到更多的支持和鼓勵。

這一點與我同為星象學家的兄弟們不需要借助魔法和巫術就可以瞭解到；也是繼「窮理查」的成功之後，更多的「窮威爾」、「窮羅賓」如雨後春筍般湧現出來，以後更不必說，還會有「窮約翰」等模仿者相繼登場。事實上，現在已經有人站出來說我們（譯者注：指以上列舉的各種「窮」字頭銜的人）只是一群頂著「窮曆書作家」名號的騙子。

在這九年裡，什麼樣的打擊我沒有經受過？情同手足的人之間也有可能針鋒相對，刀劍相向。就像正直的泰坦已經不在人世，卻有人謊稱他還在人間，甚至還被利用來攻擊自己生前的老朋友。這些人之中，不乏曆書的創作者和印刷商，而且他們做出一副義憤填膺的模樣，不遺餘力地對我進行言語攻擊。他們出言辱罵我、汙蔑我，當眾說我不是自己曆書的創作者，也不承認這個世界上有我這樣一個人存在，並且堅稱我六十年以前就死了；更有甚者，還惡意預言我將於十二個月之內死亡。此外，我還聽到很多其他自相矛盾、不攻自破的惡毒流言，所有的這些都是因為他們嫉妒我、羨慕我的成功；另一方面又妄想將讀者您對我的支持和寵愛全部奪走。

「誰知道他啊？」他們大聲嚷嚷著，「他住在哪裡啊？」但是說實話，這跟他們有什麼關係嗎？要是我喜歡過著隱世的生活，他們又有什麼權利把我拉出來，強迫我返回喧囂？我有充分的理由選擇不公開自己的住址。我想，現在是像我這樣的老人應該考慮「退隱江湖」的時候了。

我永遠都在為鄰居和陌生人找樂子，為了取悅於人，我要計算出生時刻，看相卜卦，出謀劃策，確立數字，甚至幫忙抓小偷，追偷馬的賊，畫出逃犯和走失的牛羊的行跡。上門拜訪的人還帶來成百上千的瑣碎問題：我的船可以安全返回嗎？我的母馬可以贏得這場比賽嗎？牠生下的小馬會是一匹溜蹄馬嗎？我的妻子什麼時候會死？我未來的丈夫會是誰？重要的是，我們的婚姻關係會長久嗎？理髮、修剪公雞毛、播種的最好時機是什麼時候？對於這些毫無根據、不合時宜的問題，我現在是既沒有興趣去瞭解，也沒有時間去回答。我真的已經受夠了。我發誓自己不會再去管那些憤怒的俗人，不管他們說什麼來激怒我，我也不會將自己的住址告訴他們。

我的最後一個敵人是星象學家J. J——n，在他1741年曆書的前言裡，他聲稱我前年在自己的曆書裡寫的關於他的預言都是假預言，同時抗議說我只是巴力派的一個假預言家。現在，這個被他稱為「假預言」的預言——他將會與羅馬教廷達成和解，儘管他不斷地公開聲明和反抗，但是我害怕，卻是真實地發生了。因為，在他寫的一首輓歌中，我發現有兩件事情證實這個猜測：他把11月1日叫做「萬聖節」，讀者，您嗅到羅馬天主教（譯者注：在英文中，Popery是對羅馬天主教的貶稱）的氣味了嗎？

這難道還不算是朋友之間的交好之言嗎？最顯而易見的明證是：他對

聖徒的崇拜，並且承認自己會身體力行。以下是第四頁的一句話：

無論我遇到什麼麻煩，

我會向親愛的瑪利亞呼求。

難道他認為全世界的人已經傻到認不出這些信號嗎？世人都知道天主教徒最崇敬的是聖母瑪利亞，難道他認為人們已經無知到沒有這個最基本的常識嗎？我的朋友約翰啊！你是一個不折不扣的詩人，我們都承認這一點，但是你明顯還不是新教徒。我發自內心祝福你，希望你的信仰和你的詩一樣好。

理查・桑德斯

奇怪，照理說，一個男人聰明到寫得出薩提爾（另有好色之徒含義）這樣的寓言，也應該愚蠢到把它發表出來才對。

Strange! that a Man who has wit enough to write a Satyr; should have folly enough to publish it.

有生意可以做的人，就會有錢賺。

He that hath a Trade, hath an Estate.

你明天有要做的事情嗎？今天就開始著手進行吧！

Have you somewhat to do tomorrow; Do it today.

沒有工具的工人無法幹活，不愚弄人的律師無法存活。

No workman without tools, nor Lawyer without Fools, can live by their Rules.

痛苦的布道者像蠟燭一樣明亮，燃燒自己照亮別人。

The painful Preacher, like a candle bright, Consumes himself in giving others Light.

說話和速度：緊閉的嘴巴，蒼蠅飛不進去。

Speak and speed: the close mouth catches no flies.

不要每天都去看望你的嬸嬸，不要每天晚上都跑到兄弟家拜訪。

Visit your Aunt, but not every Day; and call at your Brother's, but not every night.

雪中送炭，雙倍情誼。——拉丁語

適時提供幫助的人，提供的是雙倍的幫助。

Bis dat, qui cito dat.

金錢和禮貌造就真正的紳士。

Money and good Manners make the Gentleman.

遲來的孩子就是早到的孤兒。

Late Children, early Orphans.

拍拍自己的腦袋，班（譯者注：人名）幻想著智慧會來，但是無論他怎麼敲，也沒有任何的回應。

Ben beats his Pate, and fancys wit will come; But he may knock, there's no body at home.

好的紡車轉得快。

The good Spinner hath a large Shift.

湯姆，你的痛苦都是白費，努力再多，豬尾巴做的箭也射不到靶上。

Tom, vain's your Pains; They all will fail:

Ne'er was good Arrow made of a Sow's Tail.

海盜兩手空空，遭人白眼：他們外出尋財，歸來一身破爛，如公羊欲賣毛，最終反被剃毛。

Empty Free-booters, cover'd with Scorn: They went out for Wealth, & come ragged and torn, as the Ram went for Wool, and was sent back shorn.

人們很難忘記壞習慣和餿主意。

Ill Customs & bad Advice are seldom forgotten.

在田裡種荊棘的人，不應該光著腳去田裡。

He that sows thorns, should not go barefoot.

蟋蟀，即使是金的也沒有人要。——西班牙諺語

Reniego de grillos, aunque sean d'oro.

人生何處不相逢，山難照面。

Men meet, mountains never.

無賴們內訌散夥的時候，最終分得東西的是老實人：神父們爭吵的時候，我們終於得以瞭解真相。

When Knaves fall out, honest Men get their goods: When Priests dispute, we come at the Truth.

凱特想要湯姆，沒有人可以責怪她；湯姆不想要凱特，又有誰可以責怪他？

Kate would have Thomas, no one blame her can: Tom won't have Kate, and who can blame the Man?

貨車大，錢包癟。

A large train makes a light Purse.

人類無法賄賂死神。

Death takes no bribes.

一個好丈夫的價值等於兩個好妻子，因為物以稀為貴。

One good Husband is worth two good Wives; for the scarcer things are the more they're valued.

起床起得晚，註定奔波忙碌一整天，手上事務到了晚上也難以完成。

He that riseth late, must trot all day, and shall scarce overtake his business at night.

想要買母馬的人，往往不斷地數落馬兒。

He that speaks ill of the Mare, will buy her.

拆禮物不需要鑽頭——大材小用。

You may drive a gift without a gimblet.

晚飯吃得少，疾病少來找，藥石也就用得少。

Eat few Suppers, and you'll need few Medicines.

你如果聰明就會瞭解，觸碰別人的宗教、信用、眼睛，小心為妙。

You will be careful, if you are wise; how you touch Men's Religion, or Credit, or Eyes.

吃了魚，怎麼會還想喝奶？

After Fish, Milk do not wish.

沒有上帝，則一切皆無，有神足矣。（上帝即一切萬有）——威爾斯諺語

They who have nothing to trouble them, will be troubled at nothing.

人無煩心事，事事都無憂，最可以抵禦疾病的是自我節制的美德。

Against Diseases here, the strongest Fence, is the defensive Virtue,

Abstinence.

狗的忠誠和銀錢的標記，將是審判日的依據。

Fient de chien, & marc d'argent, seront tout un au jour du jugement.

你若作惡，歡樂消散，苦痛不減；你若行善，痛苦消退，歡樂長存。

If thou dost ill, the joy fades, not the pains; If well, the pain doth fade, the joy remains.

會犯錯的是人，為錯懺悔的是神，錯不悔改的是惡魔。

To err is human, to repent divine, to persist devilish.

人和錢，彼此扮演好朋友：人賺虛假錢，錢造虛偽人。

Money & Man a mutual Friendship show: Man makes false Money, Money makes Man so.

辛勤勞作可還債，自暴自棄（譯者注：不抱希望）債更高。

Industry pays Debts, Despair encreases them.

明亮如白晝，明媚如晨曦，克洛伊如此，實屬常見。

Bright as the day and as the morning fair, such Cloe is, & common as the air.

油嘴滑舌的人來了：恭維之間，倒背如流；謊言滿口，鬼話連篇。

Here comes Glib-tongue: who can out-flatter a Dedication; and lie, like ten Epitaphs.

希望跟紅布，是魅人的誘惑，釣魚的香餌。

Hope and a Red-Rag, are Baits for Men and Mackrel.

老去的一年與用舊的年曆，還有老病與陋習，不管多麼困難，全部丟掉。——辭舊迎新

With the old Almanack and the old Year, leave thy old Vices, tho' ever so dear.

健康長壽小竅門，以及惡性頭疼腦熱和小病小痛預防守則。

Rules of Health and long Life, and to preserve from Malignant Fevers, and Sickness in general.

吃喝要定量，視身體狀況而定，還要對心智有益才可以。

Eat and drink such an exact Quantity as the Constitution of thy Body allows of, in reference to the services of the Mind.

動腦學習的人不應該像體力勞動者吃得那麼多，因為他們無法很好地消化食物。

They that study much, ought not to eat so much as those that work hard, their Digestion being not so good.

飲食的質量要嚴格把關，找出適合自己的質跟量，並且長期保持。

The exact Quantity and Quality being found out, is to be kept to constantly.

凡事切忌過度，吃肉喝酒也是如此。

Excess in all other Things whatever, as well as in Meat and Drink, is also to be avoided.

年輕人、老年人、病人需要的飲食量各不相同。

Youth, Age, and Sick require a different Quantity.

對那些性格迥異的人來說，也是如此：對鎮靜的人而言食量太多，但

是對容易生氣的人卻吃不夠。

And so do those of contrary Complexions; for that which is too much for a flegmatick Man, is not sufficient for a Cholerick.

進食量應該（也很有可能）就是由胃的質量和狀況來決定，因為胃是負責消化食物的器官。

The Measure of Food ought to be (as much as possibly may be) exactly proportionable to the Quality and Condition of the Stomach, because the Stomach digests it.

所以，所謂的適量就是夠量，也就是胃剛好可以消化吸收，為身體提供充足養分的食量。

That Quantity that is sufficient, the Stomach can perfectly concoct and digest, and it sufficeth the due nourishment of the Body.

過量是指有些東西吃得比其他東西多，有些食物胃消化的時候比較困難，這就是過量。

A greater Quantity of some things may be eaten than of others, some being of lighter Digestion than others.

要摸索出精準的進食量十分困難，但是要按照需要進食，不能為了享受而吃，因為欲望本身不知道「必需」的界限在哪裡。

The Difficulty lies, in finding out an exact Measure; but eat for Necessity, not Pleasure, for Lust knows not where Necessity ends.

如果你想要長命百歲又身體健康、頭腦靈活，還可以不斷領略上帝的神蹟之奇妙，勞動才是最重要的。只有勞動才可以帶給你合適的胃口。

Wouldst thou enjoy a long Life, a healthy Body, and a vigorous Mind, and be acquainted also with the wonderful Works of God? Labour in the first place to bring thy Appetite into Subjection to Reason.

找出適量飲食的原則。

Rules to find out a fit Measure of Meat and Drink.

如果你進食的量影響到學習或工作，你一定是飲食過量。

If thou eatest so much as makes thee unfit for Study, or other Business, thou exceedest the due Measure.

如果飯後感覺疲倦呆滯、身重行難，這就是過量飲食的跡象。因為補充飲食應該是喚醒身體的機能，使其恢復活力，而不是令其變得倦怠消沉。

If thou art dull and heavy after Meat, it's a sign thou hast exceeded the due Measure; for Meat and Drink ought to refresh the Body, and make it chearful, and not to dull and oppress it.

如果你發現自己有這樣的病症，就要思考是否吃得太多或是喝得太多，還是吃喝都過量。如果是這樣，你應該逐漸減少進食量，直到身體的不適症狀消失為止。

If thou findest these ill Symptoms, consider whether too much Meat, or too much Drink occasions it, or both, and abate by little and little, till thou findest the Inconveniency removed.

盡量遠離聚餐或宴會，因為你如果身處其中，很難避免口腹之欲帶來的歡愉，這比遠離類似場合困難許多。除了食欲以外，你也會發現自己的其他感官欲望也是如此。（譯者注：遠離誘惑比面對誘惑再來拒絕誘惑簡單，這個準則放在任何欲望上都適用）

Keep out of the Sight of Feasts and Banquets as much as may be; for 'tis more difficult to refrain good cheer, when it's present, than from the Desire of it when it is away; the like you may observe in the objects of all the other Senses.

如果有人不小心吃得過量，就要讓他略過下一餐，這樣身體就可以自行恢復，但是不能總是這樣做，例如：他的正餐吃得過量，晚餐就要免了。

If a Man casually exceeds, let him fast the next Meal, and all may be well again, provided it be not too often done; as if he exceed at Dinner, let him refrain a Supper.

溫和適量地節制飲食可以讓人們遠離疾病困擾，遵守此法的人很少生病，就算不小心生病了，他們也可以很好地承受，很快地恢復，因為壞脾氣和疾病多數是源自過量飲食。

A temperate Diet frees from Diseases; such are seldom ill, but if they are surprised with Sickness, they bear it better, and recover sooner; for most Distempers have their Original from Repletion.

飯前十五分鐘偶爾做一些運動，例如舉重物，雙手負重活動手臂，跳躍一下，或是做一些類似的動作，讓自己胸前的肌肉活動一下。

Use now and then a little Exercise a quarter of an Hour before Meals, as to swing a Weight, or swing your Arms about with a small Weight in each Hand; to leap, or the like, for that stirs the Muscles of the Breast.

適當地節制飲食可以幫助抵禦來自外部的攻擊，助身體的免疫機能一臂之力，人們就不會輕易地頭疼腦熱、感染風寒，或是勞作之後感到疲倦。無論什麼時候身體受到傷害，或是受到外傷，或是挫傷甚至是脫臼，都可以很容易地自我療癒。

A temperate Diet arms the Body against all external Accidents; so that they are not so easily hurt by Heat, Cold or Labour; if they at any time should be prejudiced, they are more easily cured, either of Wounds, Dislocations or Bruises.

但是病毒性流感席捲村落或城市的時候，更自由地飲食才是值得提倡的。人們透過自由飲食，自身機體獲得更好的疾病抵禦能力。這個時候的疾病不是因為過度飲食而引起，而且這些病症很少攻擊吃得飽的人。

But when malignant Fevers are rife in the Country or City where thou dwelst, 'tis adviseable to eat and drink more freely, by Way of Prevention; for those are Diseases that are not caused by Repletion, and seldom attack Full-feeders.

有節制的飲食讓人們在去世的時候沒有痛苦，還可以使感官靈敏，幫助人們減緩激情以及其他太過激烈的情感。它還可以增強人們的記憶力，提高理解能力，安撫強烈的性欲，讓人們更好地考慮自己的下一個目標。

A sober Diet makes a Man die without Pain; it maintains the Senses in Vigour; it mitigates the Violence of Passions and Affections. It preserves the Memory, it helps the Understanding, it allays the Heat of Lust; it brings a Man to a Consideration of his latter End.

1743年

啊，頭腦簡單的人！你還是孩童的時候，曾經獲得兩件珍寶，那就是時間和忠告；但是現在，你已經弄丟了一件，扔了另外一件。

Ah simple Man! When a boy two precious jewels were given thee, Time, and good Advice; one thou hast lost, and the other thrown away.

友善的讀者：

讓每個人都可以從上天的護佑中獲益，是我的心之所願。但是，摘樹林裡的野葡萄來釀造美酒的方法，卻很少有人知曉。所以在這裡，我特意為他們準備一些簡單的釀酒秘法，這也是我多年以來的經驗總結。如果他們可以按照我的方法來執行，就可以釀出一種健康爽口的紅葡萄酒，而且這種酒可以保存好幾年。此外，我保證它的口感絕對不會輸給法國的紅葡萄酒。

採收葡萄應該從9月10日（先採收已經熟透的）開始，到10月底結束。葡萄採摘回來以後，需要做以下的處理：先將蜘蛛網和枯葉清理出來，然後把清理過的葡萄倒進大酒缸或是用來裝蘭姆酒的大桶裡，具體做法是：將酒桶清洗乾淨之後，敲掉一頭的蓋子，並且將它固定在另一頭上。如果有酒窖，要將酒桶站立著放置或是堆放在一起；如果沒有酒窖，要將酒桶置於屋裡最暖和的地方，而且桶底必須距離地面兩英尺[1]。

酒桶裡的葡萄沉下去之後，就要往裡面加入新的葡萄，這個過程會持續三到四天。之後，你要光著腳站在酒桶裡踩葡萄，直到踩出的葡萄汁快要淹過你的腿部為止，這大概需要不到半個小時的時間。然後你從酒桶裡出來，把沉到底部的葡萄翻到上面，再踩十五分鐘，這樣一來，就會有量

1. 1英尺=0.3048公尺。

足質優的葡萄汁出來了；但是如果踩踏的時間過長，很有可能將尚未成熟的葡萄汁榨出來，進而影響整桶葡萄酒的味道。做完這些以後，拿一條厚毯子蓋在酒桶上，並且緊密地將它包裹起來；但是如果沒有地窖，再遇到天氣比較冷的情況，就要用上兩條厚實的毯子。

透過這種方式，讓它可以進行第一次發酵，前四五天，桶內的發酵進行得十分劇烈。桶內傳出的聲音變小的時候，表示發酵開始減弱了。這個時候，要在桶底鑽開一個大小不超過六英寸[2]的木塞孔，並且每天從桶裡抽出兩次漿液，放到玻璃杯中。仔細觀察這些液體，直到它看起來像山泉水一樣澄澈的時候，才可以把所有的漿液抽出來，並且按照原來釀酒原料的量，分裝進乾淨的橡木桶（並非全新的）裡。換句話說，如果原來的大酒桶[3]裡裝有二十蒲式耳[4]的葡萄、莖葉等物，用來分裝的小酒桶至少也有二十加侖[5]的容量，這是因為每蒲式耳的原料可以產出一加侖的量。所以，你要將葡萄汁[6]從大桶裡面抽取出來，並且裝進容量適宜的器皿中，只有這樣，才可以保證第二次發酵順利進行。

你必須將葡萄汁保存在罐子裡或是瓶子裡，每二十加侖的葡萄汁會產出一加侖五夸脫[7]的葡萄酒，以下是相關的釀製步驟：

---

2. 1英寸=2.54公分。

3. Vat或是念Fatt，是一種專供葡萄酒釀製的容器，人們可以在裡面進行葡萄的踩踏，葡萄酒的第一次發酵也是在其中完成的。

4. 蒲式耳是一種計量單位，1蒲式耳（英）=36.3687公升。

5. 1加侖（美）=3.7854公升，1加侖（英）=4.54609公升。

6. Must是踩出來的葡萄汁發酵以前的叫法——葡萄汁，發酵之後的叫做Wine，即葡萄酒。

7. 1夸脫=1.1365公升。

橡木酒桶桶口朝上放置，塞著塞子，此時裡面已經盛滿葡萄汁，每天早晚各打開兩次，每次再往桶裡加入兩勺之前儲藏的葡萄汁。每次添加完成之後，用手指或勺子清潔桶塞，把葡萄籽和其他一些發酵產生的廢棄物清理掉。這樣的清理工作，需要做到聖誕節為止，到了聖誕節，就可以將塞子塞緊。到了來年的二月，葡萄酒就釀成了，除了直接飲用之外，還可以將之裝入乾淨的木桶或是瓶子裡留著以後喝。

注意：

葡萄的採摘要在露水消失之後和所有乾燥的時節進行。不要讓兒童靠近葡萄汁，因為這些葡萄汁的腐蝕性很強。如果你釀酒是為了出售，或是為了越洋運輸，就要將其中四分之一的葡萄汁過濾掉，再把白蘭地勾兌到剩下的四分之三中。按照這樣的技術來操作，收集大概一蒲式耳的葡萄可以釀出至少一加侖的葡萄酒，如果好一點，可以達到五夸脫的量。

以上的釀酒技巧，不是寫給經驗老道的釀酒師看的，主要是為那些迄今從未接觸這門技藝的新手提供相關指南。

理查・桑德斯

敢於承認自己錯誤或是勇於下定決心改正錯誤的人何其少啊！

How few there are who have courage enough to own their Faults, or resolution enough to mend them!

對有形的事物，人們的看法每天都在改變；對無形的事物，人們的看法是否就會比較一致？

Men differ daily, about things which are subject to Sense, is it likely then they should agree about things invisible?

記住什麼才是傲慢自大，球一樣鼓脹的癩蛤蟆昂首闊步向前，好像牠旁邊的蟾蜍不是癩蛤蟆似的。

Mark with what insolence and pride, blown Bufo takes his haughty stride; As if no toad was toad beside.

狗最喜歡誰就喜歡把誰弄髒，對於人們來說，身邊的不良伴侶也是如此。

Ill Company is like a dog who dirts those most, that he loves best.

在鴻運當頭的時候要謙恭明智，因為高高在上者會隕落，卑賤低微者亦會崛起。但是傲慢自大之輩從雲端墜落至恥辱深淵的時候，境地再淒涼也會無人問津。

In prosperous fortunes be modest and wise, the greatest may fall, and the lowest may rise: But insolent People that fall in disgrace, are wretched and nobody pities their Case.

法國諺語：智者只聽半句話。（有智慧的人一點就通，沒有必要聽完全部內容）

Le sage entend a demi mot.

悲傷只是徒勞。

Sorrow is dry.

這個世界上都是傻瓜和膽小鬼。然而，在厄運降臨的時候，每個人的心中都充盈著足夠的勇氣去面對，而且擁有足夠的智慧把鄰里之間的事務管理得井然有序。

The World is full of fools and faint hearts; and yet every one has courage enough to bear the misfortunes, and wisdom enough to manage the Affairs of his neighbour.

當心了，當心了！無所畏懼的人騙人的時候也是毫無顧忌的。

Beware, beware! He'll cheat 'ithout scruple, who can without fear.

滿足和財富很少碰面，你選擇財富，我寧願擁有滿足。

Content and Riches seldom meet together, riches take thou, contentment I had rather.

無論是對奴隸還是對國王，言辭之間都不能暗含輕蔑之意，因為就算是最不起眼的蜜蜂，被惹急了，也會用針螫人。

Speak with contempt of none, from slave to king, the meanest Bee hath, and will use, a sting.

教堂、國家、窮人是我們應該供養的三個女兒，少了一個都不行。

The church, the state, and the poor, are three daughters which we should maintain, but not portion off.

有時候，人們會產生無緣無故的委屈感。——威爾斯語

A achwyno heb achos; gwneler achos iddo.

對我們而言，發起一個小小的善念比透過強取豪奪和暴力流血獲得的權威和地位更有益。

A little well-gotten will do us more good, than lordships and scepters by Rapine and Blood.

借貸令人心焦。——德國諺語

Borgen macht sorgen.

讓所有人都認識你，但是不要讓人看懂你：因為人們總會蹚過淺水灘，心思淺的人也總會被欺負。

Let all Men know thee, but no man know thee thoroughly: Men freely ford that see the shallows.

提出一個大膽的解決方案很容易，但是要將之付諸實踐很困難。

'Tis easy to frame a good bold resolution; but hard is the Task that concerns execution.

寒冷和狡猾都是從北方來，但是缺少智慧的狡猾沒有價值。

Cold & cunning come from the north: But cunning sans wisdom is nothing worth.

再多的抱怨也是白費功夫，即使是一個博聞強識的牧師，九點一到，死神也會來召。（譯者注：閻王要你三更死，誰敢留人到五更）

'Tis vain to repine, Tho' a learned Divine will die this day at nine.

啊，頭腦簡單的人！你還是孩童的時候，曾經獲得兩件珍寶，那就是時間和忠告；但是現在，你已經弄丟了一件，扔了另外一件。

Ah simple Man! When a boy two precious jewels were given thee, Time, and good Advice; one thou hast lost, and the other thrown away.

迪克對他的妻子說，他要大膽發誓，無論她祈禱什麼，上天都不會讓它實現：確實如此！他的妻子妮爾說，我聽到這些話真是高興，我現在就祈禱你可以長命百歲吧，親愛的。

Dick told his spouse, he durst be bold to swear, Whate'er she pray'd for, Heav'n would thwart her pray'r: Indeed! says Nell, 'tis what I'm pleas'd to hear; For now I'll pray for your long life, my dear.

睡著的狐狸抓不到雞禽。（所以）起床吧！起床吧！

The sleeping Fox catches no poultry. Up! up!

如果你想要變得富有，就要多想想節省而不是收入：不信你看，印度群島沒有使西班牙變得富有，原因是西班牙總是入不敷出。

If you'd be wealthy, think of saving, more than of getting: The Indies have not made Spain rich, because her Outgoes equal her Incomes.

美好的德行已經敗壞。——德國諺語

Tugend bestehet wen alles vergehet.

你剛從法庭上來嗎？因為你現在的神態，明顯就是自負的神態啊！

Came you from Court? for in your Mien, a self-important air is seen.

如果想要把自己的生意做好，那就去做吧；如果不想，就把它送給別人吧！

If you'd have it done, Go: If not, send.

長久以來，天上的神仙一直在爭執的話題簡單來說就是：是這樣的，不是這樣的。就是這樣的，就不是這樣的。

Many a long dispute among Divines may be thus abridg'd, It is so: It is not so. It is so; It is not so.

經驗是一所收費高昂的學校，但是笨蛋傻瓜都要進來學習，別無他法。

Experience keeps a dear school, yet Fools will learn in no other.

1744年

掌控自己的工作，而不是被自己的工作驅使。

Drive thy Business, or it will drive thee.

敬愛的讀者：

這是我第十二年透過這種方式（譯者注：指透過曆書）來貢獻自己的綿薄之力，為了誰？當然是為了廣大的讀者朋友。如果您心地善良，願意相信我，您會知道我是在為了公眾的利益而辛勤勞作。但是你如果不相信，至少也可以接受另一個「赤裸裸」的事實——我是在為了自己的利益而努力工作。同時，也不能忘記我親切和藹的另一半——我嫻靜平和、默默付出的夫人布麗吉特，我也是為了她的利益而工作。但是不管我的辛勤勞作有沒有服務到人們，我對人們給我的幫助卻是非常感激的。在人們的鼓勵下，我生活得非常愜意，我也希望在未來還可以有幸得到人們的厚待。

我的對手J——n，J——n總是想要超過我，於是他裝作可以對未來一年做更深入的預測，並且在他1743年出版的曆書裡為讀者提供一次「免費」的預測，先我一步預言1744年的日食，想要藉機勝過我。他的原話是：「明年，也就是1744年4月的第一天，將會出現一次日全食，並且會於太陽下山以前一個小時開始出現在火星所在的白羊座。到了4月7日，在地位顯赫和身分尊貴的人之間會互生嫌隙，激發恨意……」我很替這些顯貴們高興，因為這個預言沒有成為事實。只要他們願意，他們可以一直活在愛和平安中。我要提醒他的讀者們（說真的，人數不算太多，所以影響也不算太大），不要再費心觀察這個只存在於幻想之中的日全食，因為就算瞪著眼睛看到失明，他們也看不到任何日全食的跡象。

幾年以前，我預言J——n先生將會與羅馬教廷達成和解（儘管他現在似乎也默認這種說法），為此他一直懷恨在心，於是一氣之下，給我一個「巴力的假預言家」的稱號；說實話，我始終覺得作為一個德高望重的老年學者，J——n先生的措辭是不合適的。所以，在此情此景之下，我願意將他給我的稱號歸還給他，讓他自己去處理與讀者（譯者注：此處特指購買曆書的人）之間的事情。但是讀者們可能不會接受吧，因為他的所作所為——讓自己的讀者在4月1日傻傻地瞪著眼睛，觀察那個根本看不見的日全食，他真的在愚人節把讀者們愚弄了一次。

至於大氣，他總是採用同一套老掉牙的托詞，年復一年地欺騙讀者：「沒有人可以做到萬無一失——人無完人。因為互相矛盾的事情經常同時發生，夏天的陣雨和大風總是反覆無常……」諸如此類的話。但是這些藉口難以幫助他順利解決「日全食」的風波，我也不知道他還會想出什麼新點子。

在撰寫曆書的過程中，除了額外添加一些行星起落、星月聯合的資訊，我不會再改變自己常用的表達方式。因此，那些學習意願很強烈的人，可以很容易地學到行星的相關知識，並且可以很好地辨認出不同的行星。

親愛的讀者，我是您可靠的朋友，

理查・桑德斯

獨自享用蘋果酒的人，就讓他自己一個人去抓馬吧！（獨自享樂的人，最後只會落得孤立無援的境地）

He that drinks his Cyder alone, let him catch his Horse alone.

什麼人最強大？就是可以改掉自己惡習的人。什麼人最富有？就是樂天知命、知足常樂的人。

Who is strong? He that can conquer his bad Habits. Who is rich? He that rejoices in his Portion.

男人未娶妻，人生不完滿。

He that has not got a Wife, is not yet a compleat Man.

你會是什麼樣子，做那個樣子的你就好。

What you would seem to be, be really.

如果想要擺脫麻煩的客人，借錢給他就好。

If you'd lose a troublesome Visitor, lend him Money.

說話尖酸刻薄，交不到朋友：就像是一勺蜂蜜跟一加侖酸醋相比，蜂蜜可以吸引更多的蒼蠅。

Tart Words make no Friends: a spoonful of honey will catch more flies than Gallon of Vinegar.

急事宜緩辦，忙則多錯。

Make haste slowly.

進食要少，喝湯更少，空腹睡覺會更好。

Dine with little, sup with less: Do better still; sleep supperless.

辛勤勞作、堅韌不拔、節儉樸素使財源滾滾而來。

Industry, Perseverance, & Frugality, make Fortune yield.

我可以保證，魯莽行事的人最終會怎樣？哈哈，他只能灰溜溜地逃走。

I'll warrant ye, goes before Rashness; Who'd-a-tho't it? comes sneaking after.

禱告和餵馬不會耽誤你的行程。（磨刀不誤砍柴工）

Prayers and Provender hinder no Journey.

聽理智的話，否則她很快會讓你知道她的厲害。

Hear Reason, or she'll make you feel her.

請給我昨天的麵包，今天的肉，還有去年的蘋果酒。（譯者注：麵包是昨天的好，肉是今天的新鮮，酒是去年的夠味）

Give me yesterday's Bread, this Day's Flesh, and last Year's Cyder.

上帝負責治病，醫生負責收錢。

God heals, and the Doctor takes the Fees.

懶惰（如同鏽蝕的鐵）快於勞作對衣服的磨損：所以說鑰匙常用常光亮。

Sloth (like Rust) consumes faster than Labour wears: the used Key is always bright.

微薄的收入累積起來也可以使錢包變得沉甸甸。

Light Gains heavy Purses.

讓自己遠離機會（譯者注：此處特指投機取巧的時機），只有這樣，上帝才可以讓你遠離罪惡。

Keep thou from the Opportunity, and God will keep thee from the Sin.

沒有法律的地方，人們的溫飽難以得到保障。

Where there's no Law, there's no Bread.

自滿漲，時運落。

As Pride increases, Fortune declines.

掌控自己的工作，而不是被自己的工作驅使。

Drive thy Business, or it will drive thee.

飽腹生惡念。

A full Belly is the Mother of all Evil.

可以做朋友之人，絕非善拍馬屁之輩。

The same man cannot be both Friend and Flatterer.

財富倍增者，憂慮亦倍增。

He who multiplies Riches multiplies Cares.

家中養老，如置一寶。（譯者注：家有一老，如有一寶）

An old Man in a House is a good Sign.

那些令人畏懼的人，也是遭人憎惡的人。

Those who are fear'd, are hated.

帶給你痛的東西，也讓你學到東西。

The Things which hurt, instruct.

主人幹活，用手少，用眼多。

The Eye of a Master, will do more Work than his Hand.

柔軟的舌頭可以對人們發動猛烈的言語攻擊。（譯者注：舌頭柔軟，攻擊人們的時候卻很強硬）

A soft Tongue may strike hard.

若想惹人愛，先要變可愛。

If you'd be belov'd, make yourself amiable.

一個真心的朋友是人生最好的財富。

A true Friend is the best Possession.

丈夫給喜歡罵人的妻子題的墓誌銘：這裡埋著的是我那個可憐的妻子布莉姬，現在她安息了——我也終於得以休憩了。

Epitaph on a Scolding Wife by her Husband.

Here my poor Bridgets's Corps doth lie, she is at rest, ——and so am I.

1745年

利益蒙住一些人的眼，卻點亮一些人的心。

Interest which blinds some People, enlightens others.

殷勤的讀者：

為了讓人們受益，也為了我自身的利益，現在我將為您呈上我的第十三個年終作品，希望它可以像之前的曆書一樣，受到讀者的歡迎。

上次說到星辰的起落以及星月連珠的現象，現在我將繼續這個話題，以讓不熟悉天體知識的讀者在看完以下指南之後，很快就可以學會如何區別它們跟恆星。

我們在天空中看到的所有閃閃發光的星星（有五顆除外）叫做恆星，因為它們彼此之間距離相同，與黃道的距離也相等。它們都是從地平線的同一個點上升起落下，看起來就像很多固定在天空中的發光點。

另外的五顆星星有它們自己的特殊運行軌道，因此這些星星彼此之間的距離不是恆等的。它們也因此被叫做流浪的星星或是稱為行星，即土星、木星、金星、水星、火星，這些星星與恆星之間的區別在於它們本身不發光。

五顆星星之中最明亮也是最大的一顆是金星，這顆耀眼的星星在太陽升起以前出現在天空的時候，我們稱它為「啟明星」或是「晨星」；它在太陽下山以後出現，我們稱它為「黃昏星」或是「晚星」。木星的體積看起來跟金星差不多，但是沒有金星明亮。在這五顆恆星中，最好辨認的可能是火星，因為它看起來就像一塊燒得火紅的熱鐵或熱炭，而且微微地閃著光。土星表面上看起來比火星小，色澤也比較黯淡，呈現出蒼白的顏色。水星距離太陽最近，所以很難用肉眼觀察到（譯者注：太陽的光芒太過耀眼，擋住水星的光芒）。

在1月的第6天，您可能會看到「xxx升起10 35」的字樣，這表示晚上10點35分的時候，火星會出現在東方的夜空。同樣，到了1月10日，您會發現「xxx落下7 13」，這表示金星會在10日的傍晚7點13分落下。那天晚上，如果您向西看去，可能會看見那顆美麗的星星，一直到它落下為止。此外，同一個月的18日，您會發現「xxx升起9 18」，這表示土星將於當天晚上的9點18分升起。瞭解這些行星的另一種途徑，是在它們與月亮交會的時候進行觀察，也就是：在2月的14日，會有這樣的特徵描述「xxx」，這表示月亮和土星將在那天交會。如果您於當天早上的五點鐘向外望，您會看到土星此時處於距離月亮最近的位置。類似的景象在行星升起落下以及月亮與之交會的任何時刻都可以觀測到；經由這種方式，這些行星和恆星得以被區分。

至此，我沒有其他想要補充的資訊，唯有衷心祝願您獲得世俗和精神的雙重幸福，也感謝您一直以來的厚愛，親愛的讀者，

我是隨時感激您的朋友，

理查・桑德斯

花小錢，要留意，昔小洞，沉大船。（譯者注：千里之堤，潰於蟻穴／大船沉於小洞）

Beware of little Expences, a small Leak will sink a great Ship.

戰爭帶來創傷。

Wars bring scars.

錢包輕了，煩惱重了。（沒錢憂愁多）

A light purse is a heavy Curse.

只要做好事，就會有所犧牲。

As often as we do good, we sacrifice.

一無所有的人，只能依靠自己的雙手。

Help, Hands; For I have no Lands.

對男人來說，寧願找六個假理由來應付你，也不願意說出真正的原因。

It's common for Men to give six pretended Reasons instead of one real one.

因為虛榮招致的誹謗遠甚於惡意中傷。

Vanity backbites more than Malice.

一個不會藏拙的人也是傻瓜。

He's a Fool that cannot conceal his Wisdom.

向揮霍無度的人借錢往往行不通。

Great spenders are bad lenders.

所有血脈五百年以前都是一家。

All blood is alike ancient.

即使是最好的話題，談論也要適可而止。（譯者注：再好的話題，也經不住過度談論）

You may talk too much on the best of subjects.

不懂禮數者，優點再多，於事無補。

A Man without ceremony has need of great merit in its place.

沒有痛苦就沒有收穫——一分耕耘，一分收穫。

No gains without pains.

難道是我報仇不當嗎？我從未穿裙子穿得這麼久。

Had I revenged wrong? I had not worn my skirts so long.

要麼就嫁接好果子，要麼乾脆什麼也不要做。

Graft good Fruit all, or graft not at all.

無事可做是最大的浪費。（譯者注：遊手好閒是最嚴重的浪費）

Idleness is the greatest Prodigality.

人老心年輕，壽命定會長。

Old young and old long.

把木炭摔碎，把蠟燭切斷，讓柴火熄滅。做這些事情的人既不是好主婦，也不是好主婦的朋友。

Punch-coal, cut-candle, and set brand on end, is neither good house wife, nor good house-wife's friend.

買東西的人需要有一百隻眼睛來挑選，賣東西的人只需要一隻眼睛就夠了——剛好可以睜眼說瞎話。

He who buys had need have 100 Eyes, but one's enough for him that sells the Stuff.

智者比任何一個傻瓜還要麻煩。

There are no fools so troublesome as those that have wit.

抱怨自己記性差的人很多，抱怨明辨是非能力的人卻很少。

Many complain of their Memory, few of their Judgment.

在一個人面前耍花招容易，但是要騙過所有人很困難。

One Man may be more cunning than another, but not more cunning than everybody else.

對上天，心懷敬畏和愛意；對鄰里，須得公平而大方；對自己，必須謹慎而清醒。

To God we owe fear and love; to our neighbours justice and charity; to ourselves prudence and sobriety.

愚人做大餐，智者吃大餐。

Fools make feasts and wise men eat them.

放蕩的母親讓女兒受苦。

Light-heel'd mothers make leaden-heel'd daughters.

男人的命是好是壞，要看他的妻子是好是壞。

The good or ill hap of a good or ill life, is the good or ill choice of a good or ill wife.

預防壞習慣比改掉壞習慣容易得多。

'Tis easier to prevent bad habits than to break them.

每個人都會拍胸脯保證自己的誠實，但是很少有人心思明白。

Every Man has Assurance enough to boast of his honcsty, few of their Understanding.

利益蒙住一些人的眼，卻點亮一些人的心。

Interest which blinds some Pcople, enlightens others.

買來的一盎司智慧，勝過學來的一磅知識。

An ounce of wit that is bought, is worth a pound that is taught.

下定決心以後改正的人，絕對不會立刻改正。

He that resolves to mend hereafter, resolves not to mend now.

1746年

世間最易事，要屬人自欺。

It's the easiest Thing in the World for a man to deceive himself.

親愛的讀者：

誰是窮理查？每個人都來打聽：他住在哪裡？究竟是何方神聖？但是從未有人知曉。

為了稍微滿足你的好奇心，關於我和我的夫人，不妨聽我一一道來。多虧好心的讀者和會照顧人的妻子，老天對我也不錯，由此生活快樂逍遙。我握筆寫作，她一心釀酒，或是開墾荒山，種下綠蔭。平坦的大地，留下許多條犁溝。沉甸甸的糧食填滿穀倉，累累的碩果釀出甘美果酒，印上甜美奶油，蘸上乳酪。我們讀書不少，卻很少有書可以觸動心靈，啟發智慧，帶來歡欣；美德高尚，肉眼可見，教導人們分辨善惡，識別真假。朋友真誠，男人實在，歡樂時光，相伴相隨。窗明几淨，吃喝有度，窮人羞窘，有門可入。朋黨相爭要遠離，離苦得樂愛和氣。妄信邪教眼真盲，迷信已騙幾代人。正義須作底線，規則謹記心中，手段如果偽善，良知即會迷失。善惡界限，本難分明，勿讓愚昧，再來添亂；橫衝直撞，身陷險境，無頭無腦，命葬深淵。路若選對，亦須留心，道如踏錯，護持良心。注意手段，留心動機，看準目的；自我修正，奮力修正。靈魂率性真摯，目標自由美好，光輝實在，虛偽難存：萬事順利，感恩上帝，行差踏錯，甘心受罰；滿懷希望，退隱田園，發自內心，信奉上帝。

理查・桑德斯

不到井乾涸，不知水珍貴。

When the Well's dry, we know the Worth of Water.

沒有玻璃杯的人苦苦哀求，希望可以有玻璃杯，但是有機會擁有玻璃杯的時候，最後帶走的卻不是玻璃杯，這就是人。

He that whines for Glass without G, take away L and that's he.

一個好妻子和一個好身體，是一個男人最好的財富。（譯者注：妻賢體健，夫復何求。男人兩至寶：身體棒，妻子好）

A good Wife & Health, is a Man's best Wealth.

與喜歡爭吵的人為鄰，好鄰也會變惡鄰。

A quarrelsome Man has no good Neighbours.

寬鬆穿著易磨損，緊小衣物易撐破。

Wide will wear, but Narrow will tear.

灶房起火，綾羅綢緞來滅火——送美好的禮物可以平息妻子的怒火。

Silks and Sattins put out the Kitchen Fire.

缺陷有自知之明，所以總是戴著面具遮醜。

Vice knows she's ugly, so puts on her Mask.

世間最易事，要屬人自欺。

It's the easiest Thing in the World for a Man to deceive himself.

美色與美酒，賭博與欺詐，讓財富減少，欲望增多。（色與酒，賭與騙，使財富消滅，欲望膨脹）

Women & Wine, Game & Deceit, make the Wealth small and the Wants great.

善待好心人，人人都感激。

All Mankind are beholden to him that is kind to the Good.

雙腳立地的農夫比雙膝跪地的君子更高大。（農夫雙腳立地，勝過君子雙膝跪地）

A Plowman on his Legs is higher than a Gentleman on his Knees.

美德是幸福之母，幸福是美德之女。

Virtue and Happiness are Mother and Daughter.

慷慨大方的人最不在意的是錢，但是最想要的也是錢。

The generous Mind least regards money, and yet most feels the Want of it.

人窮百樣窮。

For one poor Man there are an hundred indigent.

你熱愛生命嗎？那就不要揮霍時間，因為生命正是由時間構成的。

Dost thou love Life? Then do not squander Time; for that's the Stuff Life is made of.

良好的判斷力是一件每個人都需要，但是很少人具備，卻沒有人真心想要的東西。

Good Sense is a Thing all need, few have, and none think they want.

適當的事情正是這樣：看黑鐵匠圍著他的白圍裙！

What's proper, is becoming: See the Blacksmith with his white Silk Apron!

舌頭總是伸去觸碰疼痛的牙齒。

The Tongue is ever turning to the aching Tooth.

疏忽大意之害，甚於缺乏知識之險。

Want of Care does us more Damage than Want of Knowledge.

人們，勇敢起來吧！死亡奈何不了你，無法把你驅逐出宇宙。

Take Courage, Mortal; Death can't banish thee out of the Universe.

刺耳而不中聽，正是責備之言的真實之處。

The Sting of a Reproach, is the Truth of it.

有時候，拒絕也是一種幫助。

Do me the Favour to deny me at once.

最大的蠢行莫過於過分耍小聰明。

The most exquisite Folly is made of Wisdom spun too fine.

悠閒的生活跟懶散的生活是截然不同的兩件事。

A life of leisure, and a life of laziness, are two things.

協議無法約束暴怒的國王，粗繩無法牽制發狂的公牛。

Mad Kings and mad Bulls, are not to be held by treaties & packthread.

國再變也不能消除無能的領袖，床再換也不能治癒發燒的熱症。

Changing Countries or Beds, cures neither a bad Manager, nor a Fever.

真正偉大的人，既不會踏在懦夫背上耀武揚威，也不會膝行帝王跟前唯唯諾諾。

A true great Man will neither trample on a Worm, nor sneak to an Emperor.

裝出來的殷勤好客，開了門卻不迎客。

Half-Hospitality opens his Doors and shuts up his Countenance.

1747年

聽明人不打探秘密，誠實人不洩漏秘密。

It is wise not to seek a Secret, and Honest not to reveal it.

敬愛的讀者：

這是我第十五次用自己每年的勞動成果來取悅您，希望我們都可以因此受益。因為除了天文計算和其他曆書裡通常包含的內容——這些內容在人們的日常生活中非常實用，但是過後就會毫無價值。於是，我不斷地往裡面插入一些警句格言——讚頌美德的語句、警世恆言、智慧名言，它們之中多數雖然只有寥寥幾語，卻道出精深切要的義理，也正是由於這個原因，年輕人才會對這些話印象深刻，他們的人生也因此獲益良多，即使作為載體的曆書以及創作曆書的作者已經被人遺忘，其中的道理也不會被人遺忘。我可能會偶爾插入一兩個笑話，它們也許寓意淺薄，我必須承認，但是它們也有自己的用處，讀者可能會因為閱讀它們而感到心情放鬆，然後就會接觸到更有分量、更值得反覆琢磨的內容，所以這個部分可以被看作緩衝和小憩。每個月開頭部分出現的小詩，也是出於這個目的而存在。它們之中有很多並非出自我之手，我不需要告訴你這一點（話雖如此，但是我還是告訴您了）。如果您對詩歌鑑賞有些研究，很容易就可以看出我這些拙作只是班門弄斧。我並非一個天生的詩人，我想您也明白這一點，而且我也從未學過怎樣寫詩。再說，我實際上沒有寫詩的天分（我也學不來）。假使我真的寫了一些詩，可能也只是我依循自己的天性，寫下一些描繪星空盛景的詩句。所以，外界優秀的詩歌多如牛毛的時候，我為什麼還要將自己的拙劣之作呈現在讀者的面前？這就相當於市場上有品質優於十倍的食物在售賣，我們還把自己做的糙食拿出來招待賓客。我自己思前想後，覺得這實在不算是一個可以娛樂讀者的高明之舉。相反的，我向您保證，我的朋友們，我會盡我所能地為您呈上最好的詩作。

此外，我想要藉此良機，緬懷剛過世的雅各・泰勒先生，他生前受人敬仰，更是我們這個行業的精英。在過去將近四十年的時間裡（只有少數幾次除外），他致力於為當地以及附近殖民地的善良民眾創作曆書。他寫的曆書，是內容最棒的星曆，擁有最精確的算法，也是美國迄今為止最棒的曆書。他不僅是數學天才、星象學專家，更是偉大的哲學家，但最重要的還是他的誠實、實在、正直。願他的靈魂安眠。

我是侍奉您的窮友人，

理查・桑德斯

想要成為國內最偉大的人，你或許會因此失意；但是想要爭取成為最好的人，你或許可以成功：因為跟自己賽跑的人，可以順利地贏得比賽。

Strive to be the greatest Man in your Country, and you may be disappointed; Strive to be the best, and you may succeed: He may well win the race that runs by himself.

密林叢間無朽木，真乃怪事；親朋群裡皆好人，實屬罕見。

'Tis a strange Forest that has no rotten Wood in't.
And a strange Kindred that all are good in't.

不幸之人無人理，幸運之人不惜福。

None know the unfortunate, and the fortunate do not know themselves.

有時候需要睜一隻眼閉一隻眼，有時候需要完完全全睜大眼。（譯者注：對於某些事情，有時候可以視而不見，有時候必須計較周詳）

There's a time to wink as well as to see.

湯姆很誠實！你可以放心地把一屋子數不清的秘密告訴他。

Honest Tom! You may trust him with a house-full of untold Milstones.

他在心裡偷偷敬重好人，他就不算是太壞的人。

There is no Man so bad, but he secretly respects the Good.

勇氣促你向前衝，謹慎囑你三思。（譯者注：謹慎即大勇）

Courage would fight, but Discretion won't let him.

驕傲難去除，痛風難治癒。

Pride and the Gout, are seldom cur'd throughout.

不到身體抱恙，不察健康之貴。

We are not so sensible of the greatest Health as of the least Sickness.

身教是最好的言傳。（好榜樣是最好的說教）

A good Example is the best sermon.

父親是寶藏，兄弟是慰藉，但若有朋友，有情又有錢。

A Father's a Treasure; a Brother's a Comfort; a Friend is both.

絕望毀掉的是一些人，放肆敗壞的是很多人。

Despair ruins some, Presumption many.

內心坦蕩，縱天雷滾滾，亦能安睡；問心有愧，任翻來覆去，也難入眠。

A quiet Conscience sleeps in Thunder, but Rest and Guilt live far asunder.

若罔顧勸告，一意孤行，則無人能幫。

He that won't be counsell'd, can't be help'd.

騙人詭計要靠穿衣偽裝，真理事實卻可赤裸示人。

Craft must be at charge for clothes, but Truth can go naked.

所受傷害記沙上，所得恩惠刻石上。

Write Injuries in Dust, Benefits in Marble.

何為侍奉神明？就是對人行善。

What is Serving God? 'Tis doing Good to Man.

長期耽於一種惡習，恐會生出兩種惡習。

What maintains one Vice would bring up two Children.

一分錢的貨，買得多，也敗家。

Many have been ruin'd by buying good pennyworths.

為了多得一些而爭奪，不如因為少得一些卻知足。

Better is a little with content than much with contention.

腳底打滑好恢復，嘴快失言難收回。

A Slip of the Foot you may soon recover: But a Slip of the Tongue you may never get over.

需要耐心卻找不到的時候，才會意識到耐心的重要。

What signifies your Patience, if you can't find it when you want it.

說時間夠用的人，最後證明時間都不夠。

Time enough, always proves little enough.

聰明人不打探秘密，誠實人不洩漏秘密。

It is wise not to seek a Secret, and Honest not to reveal it.

暴徒如怪物，雖有頭顱數個，卻無智謀一點。（譯者注：有頭無腦）

A Mob's a Monster; Heads enough, but no Brains.

魔鬼給毒藥淋上蜂蜜，讓毒藥變甜。

The Devil sweetens Poison with Honey.

難以忍受別人激情的人，也難以控制自己的激情。

He that cannot bear with other People's Passions, cannot govern his own.

自己動手做，犁頭能致富。

He that by the Plow would thrive, himself must either hold or drive.

1748年

施捨得多並非真大方，明智給予才是真慷慨。

Liberality is not giving much, but giving wisely.

好心的讀者：

過去十五年以來，讀者對我辛勤勞動的成果——窮理查曆書系列——的喜愛及讚許，使我發自內心地感激。我現在要做的是盡我所能地改進某些已有曆書的內容，以期呈現給讀者更好的作品。

雖然我的朋友泰勒已經不在人世，但是他創作的星曆表（意同曆書）顯然已經深入人心，很多州的市民都在使用他的曆書，所以其實是他的遺作服務民眾，並且為他們帶來歡樂。正是因為如此，我才會冒昧地模仿他這套人們已經很熟悉的方法，而且每個月都安排兩頁紙的量，讓我添加一些有用的資訊，也方便讀者在閱讀現有版本的時候，可以與先前的曆書做比對。

當然，我沒有因為全盤接收他的方法而忘記自己的特色，我只是取其精華，吸收可以為我所用之處，並且在適當的地方始終堅持自己的特色；因此，與他的書相比，我的書在尺寸上更大、頁數更多，在內容上也更為翔實。

為靜謐的夜晚歡呼吧！

穿透這個夜空的，是我們充滿好奇的眼光，眼中所見的，是漫天的天燈，火光烈烈；以及數不清的星星，綴滿天際。

但是，你瞧！——我看見的那是什麼？

它似乎只是遠處的一點火光；從地球那方，璀璨奪目的流星也來湊熱闊：升至無涯的空間，多麼迅疾！

現在，它又越過每個天體，而且似乎對周遭很熟悉。

夫人，把望遠鏡遞給我，以便我可以看清最遠的海峽；是它——泰勒的靈魂，它正在此處遊蕩。

哦，留下吧！你這個歡欣的魂靈，留下來，白天，請帶我穿過所有人跡罕至的野境；夜晚，請帶我越過漫天繁星淌成的河流，帶我盡情領略這個廣袤的藍色蒼穹吧！

就讓我，你的同伴，讓我在星球之間自在行走，自然迷失，現在我要見識的是多不勝數的恆星，所有金光閃爍的海洋，還要追尋每顆彗星遊蕩的蹤跡。

再一次，我的繆斯女神，我的靈感又掉回散文裡，浸透全身；因為詩歌之於你，就像空氣之於魚兒，魚兒躍出水面，無水可得，只能瞎撲騰；你創作詩歌，既無靈感，又搜索枯腸而不可得，正如飛魚出水，身重行難。

有時候，我們會抱怨這個國家的冬天嚴寒難熬；但是跟這個大陸上多數的英屬殖民地相比，我們的冬天簡直就像他們的夏天一樣暖和。那片土地位於哈德遜海灣的邱吉爾河畔，北緯五十八度五十六分，西經（起自倫敦）九十四度五十分。英國皇家學會（譯注：英國資助科學發展的組織，成立於1660年）的成員米德爾頓船長曾經多次到過那裡，並且連續兩年（即1741年和1742年）在那裡過冬，他當時航行的目的主要是為了探尋一條英國通往南海的西北通道。我從他當時提交給學會的一份報告中摘錄以下的細節，即：

在九月到十月初這段時間裡，野兔、家養兔、狐狸、鷓鴣的毛換為雪白色，並且一直持續到來年的開春為止。

到了冬天，深度不足十英尺或是十二英尺（**譯注：1英尺為12英寸或是30.48公分**）的湖泊和靜態水域就會結冰，如同平地一般。這種時節，水裡的魚類都會死亡，無一倖免。在靠近海的河裡，以及深度達到十英尺或是十二英尺的湖泊中，人們可以在冰面上鑿冰開洞，穿鉤引線，整個冬天都可以捕捉到魚。但是魚兒如果被帶離水面，裸露在空氣中，就會立刻凍結起來。

初冬時節，牛肉、豬肉、羊肉、鹿肉就要宰殺得當，這樣在寒霜裡保存六到七個月也不會壞掉。同樣的，對於鵝、鷓鴣和其他禽類也是如法炮製，初冬開殺，留下毛皮和內臟，這樣就可以保證味道如初，所有的魚類也是按照同樣的方式保存。

在一些大湖大河裡，水下被封閉的蒸汽會衝出冰面，破壞冰層；岩石、樹木、托樑和我們房屋的椽子因為天寒受凍發出的爆裂聲，其聲之大，絕對不亞於舉槍齊鳴的聲響。被寒霜凍裂的石塊，脫坑而出，只留下一些大洞（**譯注：岩石之前陷於土裡造成的坑**），這些碎石塊成堆堆在一起，數量之大，甚是駭人。

如果將盛水或是啤酒的銅罐放在床邊，不到第二天早上就會被凍裂。將裝有烈性啤酒、白蘭地、濃度高的鹽水、烈性紅酒的瓶子露天放置三到四個小時，裡面的液體就會凍成硬實的冰塊。

地底下長年埋有凍土，只是不知道具體有多深；但是我們曾經在夏天花費兩個月時間，深掘到地下十英尺或是十二英尺的地方，發現依然有凍土存在。所有用來做飯釀酒的水，都是雪水和冰水；不管往地下掘多深，都找不到尚未結冰的泉水。——陸地上的所有水資源都在十月初迅速結冰，這個過程會一直持續到來年五月中旬。

房屋的牆由兩英寸厚的石塊堆砌而成；所有的窗戶都開得很小，都是由厚實的木料製成的百葉窗，而且冬天一天有十八個小時都要關死。當地人把葡萄酒、白蘭地等酒品儲存在地窖裡。每天，屋裡的爐子都要燒上四次大火才可以保持溫暖，如果壁爐裡的木材燒成炭，就要立刻用鐵罩將煙囪頂封死；這樣做可以保證屋內的熱量不會外洩，但是屋子裡的人就要受氣悶窒息的罪。

即使如此，屋內爐火熄滅四到五個小時以後，牆的內部和離床不遠的地方就會結出兩到三英尺厚的冰，每天早上都要用短柄斧頭砍掉。每天都要將重達二十四磅的鐵球燒紅三到四次，並且懸掛於屋外窗口進風處，以期緩和由窗縫漏進來的寒風；即使是這樣，一天二十四小時屋子裡大多數時間都要燒著爐子，否則啤酒、葡萄酒、墨水等液體就會結冰。

至於他們的冬裝，男人會給腳套上三雙粗毛或是粗呢質地的襪子，外面裹上鹿皮靴；再加上兩雙厚實的英式長筒襪和一雙長布襪；腿上穿著法蘭絨襯裡的馬褲；身上穿著兩三件英式夾克，外罩一件皮草大衣或是皮製長袍；然後是一個可以翻下來蓋住臉和肩的海狸毛帽，此外還要緊貼下巴圍上一條厚圍巾；在肩前的位置，還要掛著一雙紗線手套和一雙海狸毛製手套，便於他們把手放進去，手套的長度到肘部的位置。

但是即使穿著如此厚實保暖，那些在戶外活動的人如果遭遇北風，還是會被凍得要死；有些人把自己的手、手臂、臉凍壞了，全身都是水泡，以至於剛進到溫暖的屋子裡，被凍傷的皮膚甚至可以被褪掉，有些人是把自己的腳趾頭凍掉了。

待在家裡或是躺在病床上養病的人，大多會罹患壞血病，人們往往因此喪命，其中只有少數人可以倖免於難，但是只能透過鍛鍊和外出活動才可以進行預防。

冬天，北風帶來的霧大到肉眼可見，甚至可以看見其中無數的冰柱，細如髮絲，尖利如針。冰柱經常會黏在他們的衣服上，如果沾上裸露在外的臉和手，像亞麻一樣白、像犄角一樣硬的水泡就會從皮膚上冒出來。

但是如果他們可以很快地轉過身去，不要正面迎向大霧，並且可以抵抗嚴寒從手套裡伸出手來搓一搓被凍得冒泡的地方，有時候這些皮膚可能恢復如初；如果不能，他們最好立刻找到火源，並且用熱水澆洗傷處，由冰凍的空氣激起的水泡也可以因此消散下去，否則這塊皮膚很快就會脫落下來，大量熱辣辣的血清和液體也會從水泡下的皮膚滲出來；幾乎每次出門活動，這種情況都會發生；冬天，這樣的酷寒會持續五六個月的時間，在這段期間，屋外只要寒風一起，再強壯的東西也扛不住。

以上就是我從米德爾頓船長那裡摘錄的所有內容。現在，脆弱的讀者，只要有風從西北邊吹來的時候，您就會嚷著：「真是太冷啦！冷到極點了！」如果您有一天搬到我剛才提到的那個令人「愉快的」地方，您會怎麼想？或是您還是願意繼續待在賓夕法尼亞，並且感恩上帝讓您和家人都可以生於斯長於斯。

我是願為您效勞的朋友，

理查·桑德斯

人如賊者，亦需提升；小賊經常被掛上絞刑架，大盜卻經常稱王稱霸，（譯者注：竊鉤者誅，竊國者侯）但是這於你我何益？光陰流逝，尋不回。

Robbers must exalted be, Small ones on the Gallow-Tree, While greater ones ascend to Thrones, But what is that to thee or me? Lost Time is never found again.

缺乏理智的時候，需要的是更多的信念，僅此而已。

You've just so much more Need of Faith, as you have less of Reason.

天冷預防胸膜炎，天熱當心熱症流感；
不可暴飲暴食，不能過度炎熱。

To avoid Pleurisies, in cool Weather; Fevers, Fluxes, in hot; beware of Over-Eating and Over-Heating.

不信神（譯者注：一作「異教徒」）的人去世的時候，上床睡覺不點蠟燭。（寓意為：死後沒有光明照亮路途）

The Heathens when they dy'd, went to Bed without a Candle.

惡棍蕁麻一家親，你若輕摸也被刺。

Knaves & Nettles are akin; stroak 'em kindly, yet they'll sting.

1727年的本月20日（譯者注：即1727年3月20日），天文學、哲學巨匠艾薩克・牛頓爵士與世長辭，享年85歲。就像湯姆森所說，牛頓從最簡單的自然律法中追溯上帝浩渺無垠的偉大創作。他的狂喜是什麼？多麼純粹啊！多麼強烈啊！古希臘、古羅馬的光輝典範，在他的面前，亦顯黯淡。

波普先生為艾薩克・牛頓題寫的墓誌銘，因其簡潔有力又大膽莊嚴而廣受稱讚：自然和自然法則藏匿在黑夜之中，上帝說：「讓牛頓來！」（譯者注：這句寫法跟《聖經・創世紀》相似）於是，一切變為光明。

On the 20th of this month, 1727, died the prince of astronomers and philosophers, sir Isaac Newton, aged 85 years: Who, as Thomson expresses it, Trac'd the boundless works of God, from laws sublimely simple. What were his raptures then! How pure! How strong! And what the triumphs of old Greece and Rome, by his diminish'd.

Mr. Pope's epitaph on sir Isaac Newton, is justly admired for its conciseness, strength, boldness, and sublimity: Nature and nature's laws lay hid in night; God said, Let NEWTON be, and all was light.

與愚人生活，整日吃喝虛度年華；與智者同住，日夜思索探尋真諦。

Life with Fools consists in Drinking; with the wise Man Living's Thinking.

匆匆忙忙，難成好事。（譯者注：欲速則不達）

Eilen thut selten gut.

1599年的本月25日（即1599年4月25日）是奧立佛・克倫威爾（譯者注：克倫威爾出生於英國，是英國的政治家、軍事家、宗教領袖，征服蘇格蘭、英格蘭、愛爾蘭，建立英吉利共和國）的誕辰。克倫威爾的父親是一位私人士紳，他長大以後征服蘇格蘭、英格蘭、愛爾蘭三國，並且擔任護國公（有人稱其為暴君）。

其子理查雖然順利繼承克倫威爾的衣缽，但是因其性情隨和、喜愛和平，不久就從護國公的高位上退下來，成為一個隱士，直到晚年都過著無憂無慮、與世無爭的生活；直到安妮女王統治後期，理查才在他位於朗伯德街的住所裡壽終正寢。在那裡，他度過許多年隱姓埋名的避世生活，見證政府的巨大變動，以及因此而興起的激烈鬥爭，但是他已經從過去的經驗中得知，所有的這些都無法為人們帶來真正的幸福。

奧立佛曾經一度想要遷往新英格蘭（譯者注：美國的前身），他的物品甚至已經裝上前往新英格蘭的船，但是最後不知何故改變主意。如果真的到了新英格蘭，他無疑會成為一顆冉冉升起的政治新星，成為「被選中的那個人」，或是成為當地的總督，每年領著100蒲式耳印第安玉米的俸祿，也就是當時一個小殖民地總督的年俸。

On the 25th of this month, Anno 1599, was OLIVER CROMWELL born, the son of a private gentleman, but became the conqueror and protector (some say the tyrant) of three great kingdoms.

His son Richard succeeded him, but being of an easy peaceable disposition, he soon descended from that lofty station, and became a private man, living, unmolested, to a good old age; for he died not till about the latter end of queen Anne's reign, at his lodgings in Lombard-street, where he had lived many years unknown, and seen great changes in government, and violent struggles for that, which, by experience, he knew could afford no solid happiness.

Oliver was once about to remove to New-England, his goods being on shipboard; but somewhat alter'd his mind. There he would doubtless have risen to be a Select Man, perhaps a Governor; and then might have had 100 bushels of Indian corn per Annum, the salary of a governor of that then small colony in those days.

薄利多銷讓古德溫沙的店可以經營下去，也讓顧客可以陸續盈門。

Sell-cheap kept Shop on Goodwin Sands, and yet had Store of Custom.

施捨得多並非真大方，明智給予才是真慷慨。

Liberality is not giving much, but giving wisely.

挑嘴的迪克，真是可憐，受到詛咒，跟美味無緣，從來沒有享受過一頓好飯，去吃盛宴，還餓得半死。

Finikin Dick, curs'd with nice Taste, ne'er meets with good dinner, half starv'd at a feast.

唉！英雄向來都是人們捏造出來的。

Alas! that Heroes ever were made!

災難跟英雄，是交易的雙方。（譯者注：自古英雄多磨難）
然而，災難卻省下英雄揮霍的東西；
於是，災難帶走英雄，讓他們身敗名裂。

The Plague, and the Hero, are both of a Trade!
Yet the Plague spares our Goods which the Heroe does not;
So a Plague take such Heroes and let their Fames rot.

1719年的本月19日（即1719年6月19日），舉世皆知的約瑟夫・艾迪生（譯者注：Joseph Addison，英國著名的散文家、詩人、輝格黨政治家）與世長辭，享年47歲。與本國的其他作家相比，約瑟夫的貢獻更大地促進不列顛民族心智的開化和思想的進步，並且使得整個民族的禮儀提升到一個更優雅的高度。

The 19th of this month, 1719, died the celebrated Joseph Addison, Esq; aged 47, whose writings have contributed more to the improvement of the minds of the British nation, and polishing their manners, than those of any other English pen whatever.

對朋友、律師、醫生，絕對不能有所隱瞞，應該如實相告；也不能心中想著壞事，臉上卻裝作和顏悅色：如果不能看見全貌，只能窺見一斑，叫他們如何給你良方妙法？

To Friend, Lawyer, Doctor, tell plain your whole Case; Nor think on bad Matters to put a good Face: How can they advise, if they see but a Part?

這正如黑暗中騎黑豬，橫衝直撞，傷身又害己。

'Tis very ill driving black Hogs in the dark.

心生猜疑也許沒有絲毫過錯，面露疑色卻會釀成大錯。

Suspicion may be no Fault, but shewing it may be a great one.

受人保護的人是不安全的。

He that's secure is not safe.

負債經營，萬惡之首；

滿嘴謊言，稍稍次之。

The second Vice is Lying; the first is Running in Debt.

靈感之神繆斯熱愛晨光。（譯者注：早晨容易湧現靈感）

The Muses love the Morning.

蚊子（譯者注：原文為古英語「蚊子」一詞的一種拼法），或是蚊，（譯者注：古英語「蚊子」的另一種拼法），是一種體輕而小，而且有毒的飛蟲。大概50隻蚊子，還要吃得肚皮滾圓才堪到一粒穀物的重量吧！儘管如此，這些小飛蟲卻五臟俱全，每隻蚊子都擁有健全的動脈、靜脈、肌肉系統，以供其生命所有的體徵：所有的活動、消化系統的運作、後代的繁衍皆成為可能。此外，這些小飛蟲視、聽、觸、嗅、味五感俱全，由此可以想見其體內的五臟器官小到多麼不可思議的程度！這樣的構造真是令人嘆為觀止啊！這微小的生物在顯微鏡下卻如同大象一樣，看起來都是龐然大物！在屈指可數的夏日時光裡，任何一個市民，只要在自家的院子裡放上一缸水，就已經為蚊子提供足夠的繁衍條件。蚊子經常會在這些水中產卵，卵孵化之後先會變成小魚一樣的生物，之後慢慢長出四條腿和一對翅膀，接著它們會離開這些水，然後飛進你家的窗戶。

Muschitoes, or Musketoes, a little venomous fly, so light, that perhaps 50 of them, before they've fill'd their bellies, scarce weigh a grain, yet each has all the parts necessary to life, motion, digestion, generation, &c. as veins, arteries, muscles, &c. each has in his little body room for the five senses of seeing, hearing, feeling, smelling, tasting: How inconceivably small must their organs be! How inexpressibly fine the workmanship! And yet there are little animals discovered by the microscope, to whom a Musketo is an Elephant! ——In a scarce summer any citizen may provide Musketoes sufficient for his own family, by leaving tubs of rain-water uncover'd in his yard; for in such water they lay their eggs, which when hatch'd, become first little fish, afterwards put forth legs and wings, leave the water, and fly into your windows.

傻瓜會一錯再錯，錯不能改；智者會知錯改錯，終能補過。

Two Faults of one a Fool will make; He half repairs, that owns & does forsake.

哈里·斯瑪特（譯者注：smatter音譯為「斯瑪特」，當作實義形容詞用的時候，暗指對某些事物一知半解的人），口無遮攔事事說。

Harry Smatter, has a Mouth for every Matter.

與人為善，於己為善。

When you're good to others, you are best to yourself.

聰明有餘、智慧不足者，空有高談闊論，少見智慧箴言。

Half Wits talk much but say little.

傑克如果陷入愛河，就無法分辨吉兒的美醜。（譯者注：情人眼裡出西施）

If Jack's in love, he's no judge of Jill's Beauty.

傻瓜多半相信自己只是無知而非真傻。

Most Fools think they are only ignorant.

1644年的本月14日（即1644年10月14日）是威廉・佩恩（譯者注：WILLIAM PENN音譯為「威廉・佩恩」，是英國海軍艦隊司令）的誕辰。作為費城偉大的開創者，威廉・佩恩把一生的時間奉獻在為保障費城人民的自由和爭取人民應得的幸福這兩項事業上，從來沒有費盡心機地汲汲於個人名利。因為他的智慧和善良，佩恩的後代受到敬仰和優待，我們不需要因此而嫉恨他們；也因為他們自己做出的功績，以及法律的明文規定，佩恩的後人們獲得更多的榮譽和頭銜。

On the 14th of this month, Anno 1644, was born WILLIAM PENN, the great founder of this Province; who prudently and benevolently sought success to himself by no other means, than securing the liberty, and endeavouring the happiness of his people. Let no envious mind grudge his posterity those advantages which arise to them from the wisdom and goodness of their ancestor; and to which their own merit, as well as the laws, give them an additional title.

1704年的本月28日（即1704年10月28日），著名的約翰・洛克（譯者注：John Locke，英國著名的哲學家、政治家、思想家，著有《政府論》，他的理論主張被反映在美國的《獨立宣言》中）溘然長逝。至此，「微觀世界的牛頓」去世了——正如湯姆森對他的評價：他讓整個內在世界變成他自己的。

在他留下的論述人類理解的書中，很好地闡明這一點。微觀世界，正直的讀者，這是一個艱澀難懂的語詞。他們說，「微觀世界」所指的就是「小世界」，人類就被冠以這樣的稱號，因為人體這個小世界含有外在這個更大的世界具備的四種元素，等等一類的解釋。在此，我透過英語來解釋希臘語（譯者注：Greek也含有難懂之事的意思），這在我看來，要比用希臘語來解釋英語高明許多，也更容易被人們理解。但是有些作家還是堅持使用希臘語來解釋英語，並且試圖告訴我們，人類就是所謂的「小世界」，因為人類就是一個「微觀世界」。（譯者注：此處表達的效果為這類作家只是在故弄玄虛，實則言之無物）

On the 28th, Anno 1704, died the famous John Locke, Esq; the Newton of the Microcosm: For, as Thomson says, He made the whole internal world his own.

His book on the Human Understanding, shows it. Microcosm, honest reader, is a hard word, and, they say, signifies the little world, man being so called, as containing within himself the four elements of the greater, &c. &c. I here explain Greek to thee by English, which, I think, is rather a more intelligible way, than explaining English by Greek, as a certain writer does, who gravely tells us, Man is rightly called a little world, because he is a Microcosm.

1618年的本月29日（即1618年10月29日）是著名的華特・雷利爵士（譯者注：Walter Rawleigh，英國文藝復興時期的學者、政治家、軍人、探險家，曾經率領探險隊發現南美蓋亞那地區）被送上斷頭台的日子。最先指控他的司法部長官以及最後批准判處他死刑的國王永遠受後人唾罵，聲名盡毀，遺臭萬年。

On the 29th, Anno 1618, was the famous sir Walter Rawleigh beheaded; to the eternal shame of the attorney-general, who first prosecuted him, and of the king, who ratify'd the sentence.

吃什麼都可以充飢，喝什麼都可以解渴，聽什麼都覺得悅耳，看什麼畫作、雕塑、建築都覺得歡欣，任何書籍或朋友都可以讓他樂在其中，這樣的人真是幸福啊！除了美麗、秩序、優雅、完美之外，對其他任何事物都不能忍受的人，需要承受多少禁欲帶來的痛苦啊！有品味的人，其實只是口味刁鑽的人。

How happy is he, who can satisfy his hunger with any food, quench his thirst with any drink, please his ear with any musick, delight his eye with any painting, any sculpture, any architecture, and divert his mind with any book or any company! How many mortifications must he suffer, that cannot bear anything but beauty, order, elegance & perfection! Your man of taste, is nothing but a man of distaste.

姑息壞人就等於傷害好人。

Pardoning the Bad, is injuring the Good.

無法忍受別人教養壞的人，自身的教養也好不到哪裡去。

He is not well-bred, that cannot bear Ill-Breeding in others.

聖誕宴前要祈禱，當心！不要讓餐桌誘惑你，要與窮人分享上帝的恩賜。

In Christmas feasting pray take care; Let not your table be a Snare; but with the Poor God's Bounty share.

1749年

衝動過後，悔恨來臨。

The end of Passion is the beginning of Repentance.

財富與滿足，有時候同床，有時候異夢。

Wealth and Content are not always Bed-fellows.

聰明人從別人的錯誤中獲得學習，愚蠢者要自己犯錯才會得到教訓。

Wise Men learn by others harms; Fools by their own.

波以耳，在黑暗的深處，他進行最虔誠的求索，求索偉大的造物主之奇妙創作。——湯姆森

BOYLE, whose pious search amid the dark recesses of his works the great CREATOR sought. ——Thomson.

衝動過後，悔恨來臨。

The end of Passion is the beginning of Repentance.

從一個人的言辭中看出他的智慧多寡，自一個人的行為上讀懂他的意圖好壞。（譯者注：言辭彰顯智慧，行為看出想法）

Words may shew a man's Wit, but Actions his Meaning.

關於聲音的知識

佛蘭斯蒂德先生、哈雷博士以及德勒姆先生一致認為聲音每秒傳播的距離為1,142英尺，也就是傳播一英里的距離大約需要4.58秒的時間，而且

同時傳播至大氣層中各個不同的位置。需要說明的是，音速幾乎不會受到風的影響而發生改變；而且聲音無論強弱，其傳播的速度都是一致的；各種不同的聲音，例如：鈴聲、槍聲等聲音，也是以相同的速度傳播，而且自始至終都是以同樣不變的速度傳播。

Mr. Flamstead, Dr. Halley and Mr. Derham, agree that sound moves 1,142 feet in a second, which is one English mile in 4.58 seconds; that it moves in the same time in every different state of the atmosphere; that winds hardly make any difference in its velocity; that a languid or loud sound moves with the same velocity; and that different kinds of sounds, as of bells, guns, &c. have the same velocity, and are equally swift in the beginning as end of their motion.

一便士花得值，四便士省下來。（譯者注：一分錢花在刀口上，四分錢扔進錢罐裡）

'Tis a well spent penny that saves a groat.

多數狐狸變老變灰，少數幾個可以變好。

Many Foxes grow grey, but few grow good.

妄自尊大先蒙上人們的眼睛，然後讓人們開始跑。（譯者注：無頭蒼蠅，橫衝直撞）

Presumption first blinds a Man, then sets him a running.

這裡有一位女士，不喜聞見自認為產自阿拉伯的香水味。賓夕法尼亞最頂尖的鑑賞師，無法品出中國雅樂的趣味。任何一個國家的頂級美食家都很難真正享用日本精緻華美的料理。但是無論在世界的什麼地方，如果聽聞有善良和慷慨的行為發生，慈悲為懷的仁愛之士就會心生喜樂。

The nose of a lady here, is not delighted with perfumes that she understands are in Arabia. Fine musick in China gives no pleasure to the nicest ear in Pennsilvania. Nor does the most exquisite dish serv'd up in Japan, regale a luxurious palate in any other country. But the benevolent mind of a virtuous man, is pleas'd, when it is inform'd of good and generous actions, in what part of the world soever they are done.

天寒地凍過四月，五穀豐登糧滿倉。

A cold April, the Barn will fill.

知足令窮人變富，貪心使富人變窮。（窮人知足變富豪，富人貪婪變窮鬼）

Content makes poor men rich; Discontent makes rich Men poor.

Too much plenty makes Mouth dainty.

1626年的本月7日（即1626年4月7日），法蘭西斯・培根爵士（譯者注：Sir FRANCIS BACON，英國文藝復興時期的哲學家、思想家、作家）這個既偉大又卑劣的人去世了。他的偉大之處表現在其非凡的天才、高於常人的才略和學識上；他的卑劣可以經由他對一個同樣卑劣的宮廷奴顏婢膝、過分順從，以及對一個卑鄙的王子溜鬚拍馬、阿諛奉承可見一二。對此，波普對他的評價可謂鞭辟入裡：如果有才略引誘你，想想培根是多麼的光彩奪目，想想這個最有智慧、最聰明，卻也最卑劣的人吧！

培根受到世人推崇，被視為當代實驗哲學之父，這個評價確實恰如其分。有一位詩人卻對他鍾愛有加，把他人生的汙點都歸結為他陰錯陽差地選擇錯誤的人生道路：培根，倒楣的抉擇，不適合站在國家政治的風口浪尖，也不應該接觸毫無阻礙的宮廷暴行；他懷揣堅定卻容易變節的美德，鞭策自己，乘風破浪，勇往直前。在勤奮好學的庇蔭下，純良的秉性得以成型；思想深邃、涉獵廣泛、思路清晰、論斷準確、行為優雅也伴隨而來，就像由柏拉圖、亞里斯多德、西塞羅集為一體的豐富靈魂。他，這個偉大的救星！來自與世隔絕的修道院和市井平民的學校，引出真正的哲學，那個曾經長期受制於文字和形式這條魔法鏈的學問，所有的定義盡都無效：在他的帶領下，上帝之女（譯者注：真理之光）昂然向前！緩緩升起，用閃耀的指尖，再次指向天際，成串的事物，歷歷在目。

On the 7th of this month, 1626, died that great little man, Sir FRANCIS BACON; great in his prodigious genius, parts and learning; and little, in his servile compliances with a little court, and submissive flattery of a little prince. Pope characterises him thus, in one strong line; If Parts allure thee, think how BACON shin'd, the wisest, brightest, meanest of mankind.

He is justly esteem'd the father of the modern experimental philosophy. And another poet treats him more favourably, ascribing his blemishes to a wrong unfortunate choice of his way of Life; ——BACON, hapless in his choice, unfit to stand the civil storm of state, and thro' the smooth barbarity of courts, with firm, but pliant virtue, forward still to urge his course. Him for the studious shade kind nature form'd, deep, comprehensive, clear, exact, and elegant; in one rich soul, PLATO, the STAGYRITE, and TULLY join'd. The great deliverer he! who from the gloom of cloister'd monks, and jargon-teaching schools, led forth the true Philosophy, there long held in the magic chain of words and forms, and definitions void: He led her forth, daughter of HEAV'N! that slow ascending still, investigating sure the chain of things, with radiant finger points to HEAV'N again.

如果激情縱馬狂奔，就要讓理智握住轡繩。

If Passion drives, let Reason hold the Reins.

不隨便信任人，不隨便與人爭論，不隨便跟人打賭，不隨便借別人錢，這樣可以讓你一生無虞。

Neither trust, nor contend, nor lay wagers, nor lend; and you'll have peace to your Lives end.

酒不能溺斃擔憂，卻會灌溉它，助長其勢。（譯者注：借酒澆愁愁更愁）

Drink does not drown Care, but waters it, and makes it grow faster.

乞丐會證明誰才是貪戀珍饈美味的人。

Who dainties love, shall Beggars prove.

1564年的本月27日（即1564年5月27日），著名的宗教改革家約翰·喀爾文（譯者注：John Calvin，法國著名的宗教改革家，喀爾文教派創始人，創建日內瓦教會）在日內瓦溘然長逝。喀爾文和路德（譯者注：即馬丁·路德）一樣節制欲望、克己自律，甚至可能比路德更嚴格。他每年都要舉辦186場演講，布道286次；此外，他每年還會發表一本厚厚的對開本作品；再加上他長年擔任教堂管理一職，負責處理來自各個改革區、各個牧師的信件，解答疑惑或是提供建議……他很少吃肉，雖然也睡覺，但是睡得很少；而且因為把一生的時間花在有意義的事情上，所以即使只活了55年，人們也認為他活得很長壽，也因為睡覺和懶惰幾乎不能算是活著的狀態。

On the 27th, anno 1564, died at Geneva that famous reformer, Mr. John Calvin, A man of equal temperance and sobriety with Luther, and perhaps yet greater industry. His lectures were yearly 186, his sermons yearly 286; he published besides every year some great volume in folio; to which add his constant employments, in governing the church, answering letters from all parts of the reformed world, from pastors, concerning doubts, or asking ocunsel, &c. &c. He ate little meat, and slept but very little; and as his whole time was filled up with useful action, he may be said to have lived lon, tho' he died at 55 years of age; since sleep and sloth can hardly be called living.

勉強能生活，已是好生活。

A Man has no more Goods than he gets Good by.

歡迎你，惡作劇，如果你只是單身前來。（譯者注：禍若單行，不必擔心）

Welcome, Mischief, if thou comest alone.

不同的宗教就像不同的鐘錶，儘管外表彼此不一，走時卻都準確。

Different Sects like different clocks, may be all near the matter, 'tho they don't quite agree.

1215年的本月15日（即1215年6月15日）英國國王約翰簽署《大憲章》（譯者注：又稱為《1215年大憲章》或是《自由大憲章》。《大憲章》的簽署，象徵英國君主立憲制的開始），正式宣布並且建立英國自由制度。

On the 15th of this month, anno 1215, was Magna Charta sign'd by King John, for declaring and establishing English Liberty.

給年輕人的錦囊妙計：選定自己認為最棒的生活方式，然後習慣就會使它成為最快樂的事情。但事實是很多人根本沒有人生的道路，也沒有任何謀生的打算，只是每天在不同的事務中遊蕩，以致最後只能到達一個毫無價值可言的目的地。

It was wise counsel given to a young man, Pitch upon that course of life which is most excellent, and CUSTOM will make it the most delightful. But many pitch on no course of life at all, nor form any scheme of living, by which to attain any valuable end; but wander perpetually from one thing to another.

你還沒有為自己的生活——生命中的每個行動設置特定的目標嗎？

你還沒有拉開自己的那張弓，射過一支箭嗎？

或是像一個追趕烏鴉（食腐肉）的男孩

手裡拿著彈弓和石子，在樹林中來回追趕。

Hast thou not yet propos'd some certain end, to which thy life, thy every act may tend?

Hast thou no mark at which to bend thy bow?

Or like a boy pursu'st the carrion crow with pellets and with stones, from tree to tree, a fruitless toil, and liv'st extempore?

水腫病，發現要及時，

如果渾身腫起，皮膚膨脹，

叫天天不應，叫地地不靈，

再來看醫生，雖是明智之舉，卻也無力回天。

Watch the disease in time: For when, within the dropsy rages, and extends the skin, in vain for helebore the patient cries, and sees the doctor, but too late is wise.

太晚就醫，延誤時機，為救小命，寧花大錢；

醫生大夫，千千萬萬，卻無一人，能給健康。

Too late for cure, he proffers half his wealth; Ten thousand doctors cannot give him health.

可憐蟲啊，聽我一言，你要學習，學會思考：

為何發怒？原因有二：

七情六欲，天賦權利；

道德目的，人類光輝。

Learn, wretches, learn the motions of the mind, why you were mad, for what you were design'd, and the great moral end of human kind.

瞭解你自己，明白自己有幾斤幾兩，

擁有大智慧的造物主授予你神聖的使命：

做祂莊園的總管，

讓你的謹慎指引你，好好履行使命。

Study thy self; what rank or what degree, the wise creator has ordain'd for thee: And all the offices of that estate, Perform, and with thy prudence guide thy fate.

蠟製人頭，怕被曬。

If your head is wax, don't walk in the Sun.

聰明和美麗，打起人來也有殺傷力。

Pretty & Witty, will wound if they hit ye.

貧窮不是恥辱，因為貧窮而羞愧才是恥辱。

Having been poor is no shame, but being ashamed of it, is.

立志比鄰居做得更好——這個志向值得稱讚。

'Tis a laudable Ambition, that aims at being better than his Neighbours.

智者從敵人身上得到的好處，比愚人從朋友身上得到的好處更多。

The wise Man draws more Advantage from his Enemies, than the Fool from his Friends.

聽說驕傲是好人要徹底清理的「終極惡習」。

一個善變的人，總是以表象偽裝自己，有時候還會戴上謙虛的面具。如果有人因為穿著打扮整潔得體而沾沾自喜，就會有人站出來飾演反派，永遠又懶又髒、不修邊幅。

PRIDE is said to be the last vice the good man gets clear of.

'Tis a meer Proteus, and disguises itself under all manner of appearances, putting on sometimes even the mask of humility. If some are proud of neatness and propriety of dress; others are equally so of despising it, and acting the perpetual sloven.

人人都想壽命長，卻無一人願變老。

All would live long, but none would be old.

整天吵著反對驕傲的人，卻往往不是真正謙虛的表現。

Declaiming against Pride, is not always a Sign of Humility.

釋懷使痛苦消退，記恨讓傷害增加。

Neglect kills Injuries, Revenge increases them.

人們十之八九都是自己把自己害死的。

Nine Men in ten are suicides.

施行報復讓你跟對方一樣抬不起頭；選擇原諒讓你昂首挺胸，高過對方。

Doing an Injury puts you below your Enemy; Revenging one makes you but even with him; Forgiving it sets you above him.

為實用而學，大多無甚裨益。

Most of the Learning in use, is of no great Use.

空有天賦，胸無謀略，卻是不幸。

Great Good-nature, without Prudence, is a great Misfortune.

良知光明，一無所懼。

Keep Conscience clear, then never fear.

人們發起脾氣，就像瘋馬撒開蹄子亂跑。

A Man in a Passion rides a mad Horse.

讀者，再見了，願所有的歡樂都來找您；願您每年都更富有、更健康、更上一層樓。

Reader farewel, all Happiness attend thee;

May each New-Year, better and richer find thee.

1642年的本月25日（即1642年12月25日）是現代天文學和哲學之王偉大的艾薩克・牛頓爵士的誕辰。

但是與天使相比，我們引以為豪的知識又是多麼的微不足道？如果天使可以看到我們的行為，熟知我們的事務，我們的整個科學體系在他們看來一定比無知好不了多少；我們當中那些平庸的學者，基本上不可能引來天使的注目。只有偶爾出現的一兩個非常偉大的哲學家，例如亞里斯多德，或是牛頓，也許才可以用他們自己最精妙的推算博得天使展顏一笑，這似乎只是對他們絕非凡俗的娛樂活動的一種模仿（譯者注：因為牛頓等奇人天資過人，想法也許更接近「天使」）。因此，波普在下面的信中說：更高級別的存有，他們近來終於垂眼看一個肉體凡胎，正在嘗試揭露自然的法則，他們也會像人們一樣讚賞這種智慧，他們看牛頓，正如人們看猴子。

On the 25th of this month, anno 1642, was born the great Sir ISAAC NEWTON, prince of the modern astronomers and philosophers.

But what is all our little boasted knowledge, compar'd with that of the angels? If they see our actions, and are acquainted with our affairs, our whole body of science must appear to them as little better than ignorance; and the common herd of our learned men, scarce worth their notice. Now and then one of our very great philosophers, an Aristotle, or a Newton, may, perhaps, by his most refined speculations, afford them a little entertainment, as it seems a mimicking of their own sublime amusements. Hence Pope says of the latter, Superior beings, when of late they saw a mortal man unfold all nature's law, admir'd such wisdom in a human shape, and shew'd a Newton, as we shew an ape.

如何變得富有？

致富的關鍵在於節儉。每個人賺錢的能力不一，但是說到節儉，每個人擁有同樣的一種美德。

The Art of getting Riches consists very much in THRIFT. All Men are not equally qualified for getting Money, but it is in the Power of every one alike to practise this Virtue.

想要領先於世人的人，事業上也要領先別人：因為生意失敗不僅因為管理不善，還因為生性懶散，總是早上的事情留到下午做。

He that would be beforehand in the World, must be beforehand with his Business: It is not only ill Management, but discovers a slothful Disposition, to do that in the Afternoon, which should have been done in the Morning.

你尚未成年的時候學到的實用知識會幫助成年的你獲得財富，這其中寫作與記帳最不應該被輕視。

Useful Attainments in your Minority will procure Riches in Maturity, of which Writing and Accounts are not the meanest.

無論是思考性的學習還是實踐性的學習，或是普遍性的學習還是混合性的學習，都是財富和榮譽的天然來源。

Learning, whether Speculative or Practical, is, in Popular or Mixt Governments, the Natural Source of Wealth and Honour.

完美守則1：

自己行事，自己決定，僕人朋友，信任有度：作為個人，朋友公正，若為僕從，真心不多。

PRECEPT I.

In Things of moment, on thyself depend, nor trust too far thy Servant or thy Friend: With private Views, thy Friend may promise fair, and Servants very seldom prove sincere.

完美守則2：

今日任務，悉心完成，飛來橫禍，怕被耽擱；未來遙遠，虛無飄渺，財富雖美，卻也多變。

PRECEPT II.

What can be done, with Care perform to Day, dangers unthought-of will attend Delay; Your distant Prospects all precarious are, and Fortune is as fickle as she's fair.

完美守則3：

小財進出，不可大意，鼠丘雖小，堆可成山：精打細算，從無浪費，小錢省下，積少成多。

PRECEPT III.

Nor trivial Loss, nor trivial Gain despise; Molehills, if often heap'd, to Mountains rise: Weigh every small Expence, and nothing waste, farthings long sav'd, amount to Pounds at last.

1750年

不要把你的天賦藏起來，畢竟天生我材必有用。

Hide not your Talents, they for Use were made.

致讀者：

對於很多作家來說，想要流芳百世、名垂千古，是支撐他們繼續創作最有力的動機。其中少數的人已經成功地名留青史，還有一些人，他們在功成名就之後可能還會取得更大的成功，並且因為自己的作品為後人所熟知，就像古人流傳下來的名作之於現在的我們一樣；但是很顯然，這樣的作家幾乎是鳳毛麟角的。我們星象學家就像任何一個作家一樣，也是心懷抱負，孜孜不倦地追求名譽。但是經過費力的觀測和辛勞的計算，還是看到自己的作品被人當作廢紙隨手扔掉，幾乎每年都有這樣的羞辱。唯一可以給我們安慰的是，雖然它們（譯者注：代指之前的曆書）的出現只是曇花一現，但是已經比大多數同時代的作品活得長了。

但是，我們卻被指責正在重複薛西弗斯的無用辛勞：每年，我們都會將一塊沉重的巨石推向高高在上的繆斯山頂，卻無法真正到達山頂，每次快到山頂的時候，巨石就會轟然滾落，於是每一次的辛勞只是徒勞。

好心的讀者，這就是我第十七年的勞動成果。因為你們一直以來的好心支持和鼓勵，我雖然無法摘到名譽的桂冠，至少也收穫了財富，後者可能才是更好的那個。一個人活著的時候不愁吃穿，比死後留名更實際。

我在去年的曆書裡犯了幾個錯誤，有些是作者自己的錯誤，大多數是因為印刷商的緣故。就讓他們各自承擔自己的責任，坦白錯誤，修正錯誤吧！在8月的第二頁，我說28後面的幸運數字是120；這是一個錯誤，因為

120不是幸運數字；其實，28後面的幸運數字應該是496。

第一個幸運數字是6，就讓那些痴迷數學問題的好奇讀者自己去推算第四個幸運數字吧！還有一些錯誤是：有一些印刷本的3月第二頁上關於地球周長大概4,000英里而非24,000英里的內容是錯誤的，印刷的時候漏掉了開頭的數字「2」，這是印刷商的過失；在一些地方，他很吝嗇使用母音，有些地方又濫用子音，還把一首詩歌的made（譯者注：製作）一詞印刷成mad（譯者注：瘋狂的，生氣的），將另一處的warp'd（譯者注：被扭曲的）印刷成wrapp'd（譯者注：被纏住的）。就這樣，這首詩的感覺完全被破壞殆盡，只留下幾個音節用來押韻。所以，對於這些以及其他類似的錯誤，就讓讀者憑著自己的智慧和善良來決定是選擇原諒還是選擇責備。因為在這種情況下，遭受損失和傷害的主要還是讀者，如果他們第一次閱讀的時候無法領會我的真正意思，也不必指望以後還可以理解，因為他們很有可能不會再看第二遍。

印刷商確實更應該注意，不要再漏掉任何一個數字或是字母。因為如果發生這樣的情況，整個語篇的意思就會發生可怕的改變，有時候甚至面目全非。我聽說，曾經有一本新版的《英國國教祈禱書》，書中有以下一句話「轉眼之間，我們都會改變（譯者注：changed）」，就是因為漏掉一個字母（譯者注：c），變成「轉眼之間，我們都會被吊死（hanged），教眾們讀到以後，吃了不小的一驚。

善良的讀者，我從心裡祝願您新的一年，闔家歡樂。

隨時感激您的朋友，

理查・桑德斯

這個世界上有三樣東西最硬：一是鋼鐵，二是鑽石，三是認識自己。

There are three Things extreamly hard: Steel, a Diamond and to know one's self.

飢餓是最好的開胃鹹菜。

Hunger is the best Pickle.

善於控制自己激情的人可以管理別人，受到激情支配的人只能為人所使。

He is a Governor that governs his Passions, and he a Servant that serves them.

一分神秘與謙遜，為其他的特點與美德增色十分。

A Cypher and Humility make the other Figures & Virtues of ten-fold Value.

若非為填口腹欲，早已身披黃金衣。（譯者注：吃喝花銷大，錢財難聚集）

If it were not for the Belly, the Back might wear Gold.

欲挫敵人勇，先察自己身。

Wouldst thou confound thine Enemy, be good thyself.

驕傲自負就像乞丐高聲乞討，只會更顯粗俗，招人厭惡。

Pride is as loud a Beggar as Want, and a great deal more saucy.

還清你欠下的，你就會知道自己價值多少。

Pay what you owe, and what you're worth you'll know.

悔恨毫無用處，只會增加罪惡感。

Sorrow is good for nothing but Sin.

很多人自認為買到了快樂，其實他只是把自己賣給快樂做奴隸。

Many a Man thinks he is buying Pleasure, when he is really selling himself a Slave to it.

要嫁接就嫁接好果樹，不然就什麼都不要做。

Graft good Fruit all, or graft not at all.

貧窮但是可以保持正直，這很難做到（但是很光榮）：空袋子，立不起來，有朝一日站起來，既結實又有力。

'Tis hard (but glorious) to be poor and honest: An empty Sack can hardly stand upright; but if it does, 'tis a stout one!

可以坦然接受別人批評並且及時改正錯誤的人，即使不是智者，也已經走在通往智慧的道路上。

He that can bear a Reproof, and mend by it, if he is not wise, is in a fair way of being so.

人無美德，亦無歡樂。

Beatus esse sine Virtute, nemo potest.

再有益的教義，說給羔羊聽，也是左耳進右耳出；再稱職的牧師，向人們布道，也無法教人們節制改過。

Sound, & sound Doctrine, may pass through a Ram's Horn, and a Preacher, without straitening the one, or amending the other.

指責我的過失以前，先把你的手指洗乾淨。

Clean your Finger, before you point at my Spots.

蘭姆酒灑了，只是喝不到酒而已；如果喝到肚子裡，卻經常酒沒人也沒。

He that spills the Rum, loses that only; He that drinks it, often loses both that and himself.

書寫真是絕妙的發明啊！一個人可以藉由書寫跟1,000里格[1]以外的人交流，不需要張口說話，只需要借助22個字母，就可以言及遙遠的年代，還可以獲得5,852,616,738,497,664,000種不同的組合，更可以在一個極其狹小的羅盤上表達出所有的事情。遺憾的是，發明這種偉大藝術的人卻無法青史留名，供後人瞻仰。

What an admirable Invention is Writing, by which a Man may communicate his Mind without opening his Mouth, and at 1,000 Leagues Distance, and even to future Ages, only by the Help of 22 Letters, which may be joined 5,852,616,738,497,664,000 Ways, and will express all Things in a very narrow Compass. 'Tis a Pity this excellent Art has not preserved the Name and Memory of its Inventor.

事多難免出錯。

Those that have much Business must have much Pardon.

---

1. 1里格≈4,828公尺。

換床睡覺治不好發熱，換一門生意無法消除煩惱。

Discontented Minds, and Fevers of the Body are not to be cured by changing Beds or Businesses.

斧頭雖小，砍樹會倒。

Little Strokes, fell great Oaks.

精明可以應付一時，卻無法應付一輩子。

You may be too cunning for One, but not for All.

天才沒有受過教育，就像白銀還在礦裡。

Genius without Education is like Silver in the Mine.

很多人靠小聰明混日子，只是終有一日，聰明不足反受累。

Many would live by their Wits, but break for want of Stock.

人窮心正直，死後一身輕。

Poor Plain dealing! Dead without Issue!

你可以忍受自己的過錯，為何不能容忍自己妻子的缺點？

You can bear your own Faults, and why not a Fault in your Wife?

儘管謙虛是美德，太過忸怩卻是錯。

Tho' Modesty is a Virtue, Bashfulness is a Vice.

不要把你的天賦藏起來，畢竟天生我材必有用。

Hide not your Talents, they for Use were made.

日晷放在樹蔭裡，還叫什麼日晷！

What's a Sun-Dial in the Shade!

如果不瞭解事物的本質，就算知道名稱又有什麼用？

What signifies knowing the Names, if you know not the Natures of Things?

提姆學識淵博，說「馬」會用九種語言，同時也很無知，要騎馬卻買牛。

Tim was so learned, that he could name a Horse in nine Languages; So ignorant, that he bought a Cow to ride on.

當下永遠不是黃金時代。

The Golden Age never was the present Age.

以你的家族為榮，那是恥辱！家族以你為榮，才是光榮。

'Tis a Shame that your Family is an Honour to you! You ought to be an Honour to your Family.

玻璃、瓷器、美名，破碎容易修復難。

Glass, China, and Reputation, are easily crack'd, and never well mended.

1751年

思想懶惰比身體懶惰更可怕。

There are lazy Minds as well as lazy Bodies.

敬愛的讀者：

占星學是最古老的科學之一，古時候很受智者及偉人的推崇。如果沒有先請示詢問占星師的意見，古時候的國王不會貿然發動戰爭或是議和，將軍也不敢隨便與敵軍交手開戰；總之就是，占星師沒有事先研究星象變化和天體聚合狀況，標示萬事順遂的黃道吉日，任何重要的事務都會難以成行。但是如今這門高貴的藝術（尤其讓我們生活的這個時代汗顏！）已經跌落至受人輕視的谷底；大人物們已經不再重視我們的作用，國家結盟，議會立法，也不再徵求我們的意見；除了幫忙找出採收玉米糧食或是閹割小豬的最佳時機以外，我們當初辛苦得來的學識現在已經毫無用武之地。

但是，這個「惡作劇」的起因很大程度上歸咎於我們自己：因為如果不是我們之中的某些人極力鼓動無知的群眾，他們絕對不敢貶低我們占卜口諭的價值。然而，繆斯女神已經遭到愛子們的背叛，那些承蒙她恩賜而習得這門神聖藝術的人毫不留情地背叛她；現代天文學界最負盛名的泰斗們，牛頓們、哈雷們、惠斯登們昧著良心肆意地謾罵她、侮辱她。這些人之中，只有最後一個天文學家——惠斯登，在其活著的時候對此進行懺悔，直言不諱，說出自己的心裡話。他前期的作品總是視司法認可的權威性占星術為幻想空談，聲稱恆星和行星（太陽和月亮除外）之間的距離極其遙遠，因此不可能對地球造成影響，而且也不可能根據星象的位置做出任何預測。

但是在1749年出版的回憶錄中，82歲的惠斯登在此書的第607頁預言土耳其帝國、奧地利王國、德意志帝國等國的分崩離析和羅馬教宗制度的崩壞，以及猶太人的復興和千禧年都會在1766年到來。而且，這不僅可以從《聖經》預言中查驗到，還有（用他自己的話來說）「顯著的天文信號也警示人類有事情要發生。」即：1715年開始出現的北極光；在新教改革期間，與過去的十一年之中出現的七次彗星事件（分別是1737年、1739年、1742年、1743年、1744年、1746年、1748年七次）相比，1530年、1531年、1533年、1534年這四年之中，總共出現六次彗星。

還有自1748年7月14日出現的大型日環食，這次日環食的中心穿過蘇格蘭至東印度群島的四個君主國。從去年七月的月食開始，月亮周圍每隔幾個月就會出現昴宿星蝕，這種現象一直持續大概三年。在這段期間，羅馬全境都可以看見以上的星象變化，與以賽亞預言西元前590年至西元前595年這六年之間會出現的畢宿星團星蝕如出一轍。1753年4月25日出現的水星凌日現象，在整個羅馬帝國都可以看見。1456年、1531年、1607年、1682年出現的彗星，還會於1757年年末或是1758年年初再次出現，屆時，整個羅馬帝國的民眾都可以看見。發生於1761年5月26日的金星凌日現象，同樣也可以被羅馬帝國各個角落的人們看見。最後，羅馬全境在1764年3月11日會發生一次日全食。透過觀測計算這些天文跡象，惠斯登預言此後16年將要發生的重要事件。

有話為證：「千禧年或是叫做基督統治的千年即將拉開序幕，屆時新的天堂和地球樂園將會來臨；基督的世界中，不會再有異教徒的存在（出自此書的第398頁），坦布里奇也不再會有賭桌和賭博！」

如果這些預言得以成真，將是對我們占星學這門藝術一個最有力的證明；但是如果預言不幸失敗，毫無疑問，學識淵博的天文學家如惠斯登者，也是可以另闢蹊徑，找出其他星象變化，並且預告世人：「異教徒的皈依會有所延遲，千禧年也會延期到來。」既然已經有人對這類重大事件做出預言，此後還有誰會懷疑我們對下雨還是出太陽這類小事的預言能力？讀者，再會了，希望您可以善加利用這一年的時間和您手中的曆書，因為您看，如果按照惠斯登的說法發展，您最多只能擁有十六本曆書。

理查・桑德斯

波多馬克，1750年7月30日

請不要燒我的房子來烤你的雞蛋。

Pray don't burn my House to roast your Eggs.

有些事情值得爭論一番，有些朋友值得深入瞭解；以自己的美德去推想敵人的美德。

Some Worth it argues, a Friend's Worth to know; Virtue to own the Virtue of a Foe.

興旺發達時易察覺惡習，痛苦逆境中常看見美德。

Prosperity discovers Vice, Adversity, Virtue.

鐘聲敲響一下：我們毫不在意，卻對時間的流逝一無所知。人有舌頭，就有智慧。若是聽到這樣的話「沒事，沒事，那是我們終將逝去的時光」；但是它們現在在哪裡？洪流肆虐之後的歲月：時間發出催促的信號；那麼，要多少錢才可以完成？

把握今日，明智利用，拖延至瘋；明天，索命之神將要臨到；如此這般，直到生命的智慧被擠乾：「拖延」是盜走時間的賊，年復一年，時間被一點一點地偷走，即使只留下一瞬間的憐憫，卻也成為人生永恆的景致。但是如果這樣的場景不經常出現，豈不是很奇怪嗎？但要是太經常出現，又更加奇怪了。

The Bell strikes One: We take no Note of Time, but from its Loss. To give it then a Tongue is wise in Man. If heard aright it is the Knell of our departed

Hours; Where are they? With the Years beyond the Flood: It is the Signal that demands Dispatch; How much is to be done?

Be wise Today, 'tis Madness to defer; Next day the fatal Precedent will plead; Thus on, till Wisdom is push'd out of Life: Procrastination is the Thief of Time, Year after Year it steals till all are fled, and to the Mercies of a Moment leaves the vast Concerns of an eternal Scene. If not so frequent, would not this be strange? That 'tis so frequent, This is stranger still.

如果一個人擁有的產業過多，他的處境只會更糟。

Many a Man would have been worse, if his Estate had been better.

我們可以提供意見，但是不要越俎代庖。

We may give Advice, but we cannot give Conduct.

自己馬褲上有臭味，看到別人鼻子一皺，心中就會一咯噔。

He that is conscious of a Stink in his Breeches, is jealous of every Wrinkle in another's Nose.

有很多方法治療相思病和牙痛，但是管用的是擁有和剝奪。

Love and Tooth-ach have many Cures, but none infallible, except Possession and Dispossession.

思想懶惰比身體懶惰更可怕。

There are lazy Minds as well as lazy Bodies.

小恩小惠，銘感五內，時間一到，即刻報答；更大恩惠，千恩萬謝，嘴上說說，人人知曉；大恩大德，得魚忘筌，厚顏無恥，貪得無厭。

Most People return small Favours, acknowledge middling ones, and repay great ones with Ingratitude.

一心鍾情於穿衣打扮，是空洞無用的；不要只顧眼前欲望，要先問錢包是否可以承受。

Fond Pride of Dress is sure an empty Curse; E're Fancy you consult, consult your Purse.

年輕的時候積極卻浮躁，上了年紀變得謙遜卻多疑：所以穀物未熟隨風盪，身姿挺直無負擔，待到穗壓枝頭，穀粒飽滿成熟之時，腦袋只能沉沉下垂。

Youth is pert and positive, Age modest and doubting: So Ears of Corn when young and light, stand bolt upright, but hang their Heads when weighty, full, and ripe.

壓住先起的欲望，比滿足後來的欲望容易得多。

'Tis easier to suppress the first Desire, than to satisfy all that follow it.

判斷一個人的財富多寡，敬神與否，不能只從星期日的外在表現來看。

Don't judge of Mens Wealth or Piety, by their Sunday Appearances.

拜訪朋友增進情誼，但是不能太頻繁。

Friendship increases by visiting Friends, but by visiting seldom.

如果你的財富屬於你，你為何不帶著它們一起到另一個世界？

If your Riches are yours, why don't you take them with you to the t'other World?

比黃金更有價值的是什麼？鑽石。比鑽石更寶貴的是什麼？美德。

What more valuable than Gold? Diamonds. Than Diamonds? Virtue.

今天是明天的學生。

Today is Yesterday's Pupil.

如果俗世的物品不能救我免死，它們同樣不能阻礙我獲得永生。

If worldly Goods cannot save me from Death, they ought not to hinder me of eternal Life.

跟朋友說自己的錯誤需要很多信心，但是指出他的錯誤需要更多的信心。

'Tis great Confidence in a Friend to tell him your Faults, greater to tell him his.

貪婪費盡心機積攢下來的，卻經常被野心傻傻地揮霍。

Ambition often spends foolishly what Avarice had wickedly collected.

賓格身陷官司難自拔，有朝一日對簿公堂，直到他使用「與格」，律師才明瞭。

Pillgarlic was in the Accusative Case, and bespoke a Lawyer in the Vocative, who could not understand him till he made use of the Dative.

大輪船可歷險，小扁舟靠岸邊。

Great Estates may venture more; Little Boats must keep near Shore.

嘴巴刁鑽，吃什麼都不香。

Nice Eaters seldom meet with a good Dinner.

不盯著工人幹活，就是把你的錢包打開。

Not to oversee Workmen, is to leave them your Purse open.

智者和勇士都敢於認錯。

The Wise and Brave dares own that he was wrong.

狡猾的人往往沒有能力。

Cunning proceeds from Want of Capacity.

自負的人討厭自以為是——當然，是別人的自以為是。

The Proud hate Pride——in others.

評價一個人，誰可以做得最好，是他的敵人還是他自己？

Who judges best of a Man, his Enemies or himself?

喝醉乃萬惡之首，有人因為酒變成傻子，有人因為酒變成野獸，還有一些，變成惡魔。

Drunkenness, that worst of Evils, makes some Men Fools, some Beasts, some Devils.

如果在神聖的節日裡沒有虔誠的心，就不是節日。

'Tis not a Holiday that's not kept holy.

越可以忍耐的好脾氣，將要忍受得就會越多。

A Temper to bear much, will have much to bear.

好心的讀者：

國王和議會都認為是時候修改我們的日曆年，所以就從1752年9月裡抽走11天，並且規定以後都要將1月1日作為新一年的開始，於是我打算將過去到現在（迄今為止）日曆年發生的變化以及改變的原因向您介紹，或許可以稍微滿足一點您的好奇心。

季節的交替變化，似乎是第一份日曆年年例法規制定的理由。人們自然會心生好奇，也很想知道季節變化多樣性的原因，很快人們就發現，這是由地球距離太陽的遠近造成的；在這個基礎上，地球繞著那個發光體——太陽完整運行一周，最後又回到自己軌道上原來的位置，人們將這段時間叫做「太陽年」。

因此，季節就成為「年（譯者注：日曆年、太陽年）」的主要制定依據，他們最關注的是日曆年的相同時段應該總是對應相同的季節；也就是說，每個太陽年開始的時候，地球應該位於其軌道上的同一個位置；而且它們彼此保持同步，同時轉彎，也同時結束。

在不同的國家，對年的劃分方式也是不同的，劃分的點起始於黃道十二宮的不同位置，甚至對太陽的運行時間的規定也是不同的。這樣的結果是：有些國家的曆書比其他國家的曆書更準確和完善，但是沒有哪個國家的曆書是足夠精確的；也就是說，沒有哪種曆法可以完全對應太陽運行的軌跡。

正是埃及人，或許我們應該將功勞歸給希羅多德（譯者注：Herodotus，古希臘作家、歷史學家，被稱為「歷史之父」），最先制定並且啟用年份。當時規定的一年有360天，總共劃分為12個月，每個月有30天。

水星崔斯默圖又給這種劃分另添了5天。據說，泰利斯（譯者注：古希臘哲學家）就是在這個基礎上制定希臘的曆書，儘管這份曆書沒有在當時的希臘廣泛傳播。其他的，例如：猶太人、敘利亞人、羅馬人、波斯人、衣索比亞人、阿拉伯人的曆書也是各有千秋。

實際上，考慮到當時星象學家（譯者注：亦作天文學家）可憐的社會地位，也難怪不同的人會對地球運行週期的計算抱持不同的態度。甚至狄奧多羅斯（譯者注：古希臘歷史學家）、普魯塔克（譯者注：羅馬帝國時代希臘作家、哲學家、歷史學家）、普林尼也向我們保證埃及後來的曆書跟最初的相比，已經發生很大的變化。

根據我們的計算，太陽年或是地球穿過十二黃道宮而運行一周最後回到起始點的時間間隔為365天5小時49分鐘。儘管有些天文學家有時候會少算幾秒鐘或是一分鐘的時間，例如：天文學家克卜勒的計算結果是365天5小時48分57秒39毫秒，里喬利（譯者注：義大利天文學家喬瓦尼・巴蒂斯塔・里喬利 Giovanni Battista Riccioli）算得是365天5小時48分鐘，第谷・布拉赫（譯者注：丹麥天文學家、占星師）的結果是365天5小時48分鐘。

民用年是各個國家用來計算時間流逝的曆書法規，或是可以將這個民用年看作由一定數量的整天組成的回歸年；無論是小時還是分鐘的零頭全部被省略，這樣一來，人們在日常生活中更容易計算時間。

因此，一個回歸年是365天5小時49分鐘，一個民用年是365天，又因為必須與天體運行保持統一步調，才可以保證曆書的準確性，所以每隔四年，一年必須有366天。如果每年多餘出來的時間剛好是6個小時，曆書就不會出錯了。

古羅馬的曆法是由羅穆盧斯（譯者注：戰神Mars之子，與其兄弟Remus瑞摩斯同為羅馬城的建造者）訂立的，這份曆法只有十個月，即：I.三月31天，II.四月30天，III.五月31天，IV.六月30天，V.七月31天，VI.八月30天，VII.九月30天，VIII.十月31天，IX.十一月30天，X.十二月30天，總共是304天，比一個太陽年少61天。

因此，羅穆盧斯曆法對每年開端的規定是不清晰的，而且不能固定地跟季節相對應。為了避免這樣的不便，當時的皇帝每年都會下令增加許多天數，以便節令可以跟第一個月相對應，但是不在曆法中做出實質性的修改，也不把這些增加的天數放在一起，合併為一個月。

努瑪・龐皮留斯（譯者注：羅馬王政時期第二任國王）對這種毫無規範的曆法進行改正，他的做法是：將前一年添加的日子合併起來，組成兩個新的月份——一月和二月。這樣一來，努瑪的曆法就有12個月，它們分別是：I.一月29天，II.二月28天，III.三月31天，IV.四月29天，V.五月31天，VI.六月29天，VII.七月31天，VIII.八月29天，IX.九月29天，X.十月31天，XI.十一月29天，XII.十二月29天。全年共計355天，比一個太陽年少10天，但是這種曆法規定的開端還是不夠清晰，也不夠確定。

然而，努瑪還是想要讓曆法跟冬至相對應，於是他下令要每隔兩年在二月增加22天，每隔四年變作23天，每隔六年增加的日子是22天，每隔八年增加的天數是23天。

但不幸的是，這項規定沒有讓問題得到順利解決，只是使用新的方法增加天數；而且跟每隔八年要增加23天的目標相反，最終增加的天數只有15天。本來應該體恤關照萬民的祭司長，或是稱為大祭司，卻辜負眾人的信任，把事情弄得一團糟。之後，羅馬人的曆法就按照這樣的模式延續下去，直到尤利烏斯・凱撒（譯者注：羅馬共和國末期傑出的軍事統帥、政治家，也是羅馬帝國的奠基者）對它進行徹底的改革，並且創設儒略曆（譯者注：Julian Year）。

儒略年是一種太陽年，一般包含365天，規定每隔四年就有一個閏年，閏年是366天。儒略曆中月份的叫法、排列方式，以及每個月的天數跟我們長久以來使用的曆書規定的一致，所以我們很熟悉。

因此，按照天文計數，一個儒略年有365天6小時，比一個真正的太陽年還要長11分鐘，由此，每131年就會多出一個整天。自此，羅馬曆法開始沿用儒略曆，直到教宗額我略十三世改革為止。

尤利烏斯・凱撒在制定曆法的時候，著名數學家索西琴尼（譯者注：希臘著名的天文學家）特意從埃及趕來協助改革。索西琴尼將大祭司誤漏的67天重新補進曆書裡，並且規定把冬至日作為一年的起始日，這樣一來，一年就會由15個月或是445天組成，也因此曾經被叫做「混亂年」。

直到16世紀中期，所有的基督教國家都使用這種曆法，之後有幾個國家還在使用；這種情況一直持續到瑞典、丹麥、英國開始使用格里曆為止；但是實際上，英國是到了第二年的9月2日（譯者注：即以上提到的國家開始使用格里曆之後的第二年）才停止使用「混亂曆書」。

格里曆按照以下的方式將儒略曆進行改正：以前是每隔一百年才有一次閏年，新曆法經過改正之後規定，連續的四年中，前三年為普通年，只有第四年是閏年。

儒略年出現的11分鐘之誤差雖然很小，但是隨著時間流逝，誤差的時間也會逐漸積少成多，最後變成極其可觀的誤差；從凱撒進行曆法的修訂開始，已經累積13天的誤差，讓春秋日的分界受到很大的干擾。為了改正這個不斷變大的誤差，教宗額我略十三世召集當時最有名望的天文學家，讓他們著手修正儒略曆。於是，為了恢復春秋分的時間規定，他們將尼斯議會上得到的十天廢除，即讓10月的5日變成10月的15日。

西元1700年的時候，10天的誤差增加到11天。為了預防進一步的混亂發生，德國這個新教國家接受並且開始使用格里曆。如今到了1752年，英國也以他們為榜樣，開始使用格里曆。

但是，格里曆距離完美的稱號還很遠，因為我們之前已經提到，經過四個世紀的時間，儒略年會多出3天1小時20分鐘；但是如果按照格里曆的演算法，經過同樣長度的時間，格里曆中只會保留3天，剩下的1小時20分鐘要經過72個世紀的累積疊加，才會達到一個整天的時間。

至於曆書的開始日，英國的法定曆書規定要從聖母報恩日，也就是3月的第25天開始算起，儘管歷史上的新年伊始日是耶穌受割禮的日子，也就是我們熟知的1月1日。義大利與德國都是以每年的1月1日為新年，我們國家今後也是一樣，國會已經通過法案，宣布從1752年開始，每年的1月1日都是新年伊始。

法案通過以後，貴格會教友們就向自己的鄰國提議使用這種曆法一事，在倫敦舉行的年度會議上達成一致意見，提議包括將9月抽走11天，並且規定以後的1月1日是新年的開始；從今以後，「January」就成為真正意義上的一月——每一年的第一個月。其餘的月份也依次按照自己的編號和順序進行排列，所以才有今天的「September」（譯者注：九月）——一年之中的第九個月，「December」（譯者注：十二月）——一年之中的第十二個月，等類似的觀念。

總而言之，這份國會法案包含很多重要的事項，並且會在不久的將來傳遍英國殖民地的各個角落。所以，為了讓讀者們高興，我特意做出以上的詳細解讀。按照往年慣例，我在此送上新年的祝福（這確實是新的一年，是一個我們之前從未見過，以後也不會再見到的新年），祝願所有的讀者新年快樂。

我是您忠實的僕人，

理查·桑德斯

他回溯過去的時候，盡是溢美之詞，好像在盡力兜售什麼似的。

Observe old Vellum; he praises former Times, as if he'd a mind to sell 'em.

國王的手臂夠長，但是厄運的手臂更長：所以，不要妄想逃出厄運的五指山。

Kings have long Arms, but Misfortune longer: Let none think themselves out of her Reach.

缺了釘子，丟了馬掌；缺了馬掌，失了馬兒；少了馬兒，騎馬的人也就不見了。

For want of a Nail the Shoe is lost; for want of a Shoe, the Horse is lost; for want of a Horse the Rider is lost.

忙碌的人少有閒客拜訪；沸騰的鍋沒有蒼蠅光臨。

The busy Man has few idle Visitors; to the boiling Pot the Flies come not.

禍福皆是真正的試金石。

Calamity and Prosperity are the Touchstones of Integrity.

鋪張浪費通常比狼貪虎視更有損公正。

The Prodigal generally does more Injustice than the Covetous.

慷慨大方的人同為一家。

Generous Minds are all of kin.

與復仇造成的傷害相比，寬恕更高尚，鄙視更有氣概。

'Tis more noble to forgive, and more manly to despise, than to revenge an Injury.

兄弟不一定是朋友，但是朋友卻一定是兄弟。

A Brother may not be a Friend, but a Friend will always be a Brother.

卑鄙是傲慢的來源。

Meanness is the Parent of Insolence.

人類是一種非常奇怪的動物：一半在譴責自己的作為，一半又在按照自己譴責的方式行事；至於剩下的，說是說的，做是做的。

Mankind are very odd Creatures: One Half censure what they practise, the other half practise what they censure; the rest always say and do as they ought.

嚴厲通常意味著寬厚，寬厚通常意味著嚴厲。

Severity is often Clemency; Clemency Severity.

有求必應如果太快，要求很快又會找上門。

Bis dat qui cito dat: He gives twice that gives soon; i. e. he will soon be called upon to give again.

越可以忍耐的好脾氣，將要忍受得就會越多。

A Temper to bear much, will have much to bear.

驕傲吃名為虛榮的午餐，喝叫做蔑視的湯。

Pride dines upon Vanity, sups on Contempt.

偉大的功績和無比的自豪都是靦腆的。

Great Merit is coy, as well as great Pride.

一個不孝的女兒會成為一個難以管教的妻子。

An undutiful Daughter, will prove an unmanageable Wife.

大人和小孩都有屬於自己的玩具，不同只在於價格。

Old Boys have their Playthings as well as young Ones; the Difference is only in the Price.

脾氣太過順從，其實是跟自己過不去。

The too obliging Temper is evermore disobliging itself.

吃飯之前需要把事情做完，因為肚子飽了，腦袋就會懶得思考，身體也會懶得動。

Hold your Council before Dinner; the full Belly hates Thinking as well as Acting.

勇敢的人和有智慧的人都心懷慈悲，懦夫和傻子經常冷漠無情。

The Brave and the Wise can both pity and excuse; when Cowards and Fools shew no Mercy.

虛禮不是禮貌，客套也不是禮節。

Ceremony is not Civility; nor Civility Ceremony.

想要實現一半的心願，麻煩就會加倍找上門。

If Man could have Half his Wishes, he would double his Troubles.

木匠的工具壞了可不是鬧著玩的，醫生的工具壞了後果更嚴重。

It is ill Jesting with the Joiner's Tools, worse with the Doctor's.

孩子跟王子一樣，都會為了小事爭吵。

Children and Princes will quarrel for Trifles.

讚美給了不配得到讚美的人，對被讚美的人而言是很嚴重的詆毀。

Praise to the undeserving, is severe Satyr.

成功毀掉了許多人。

Success has ruin'd many a Man.

驕傲自負跟卑鄙低劣之間距離很近，只隔著一張薄薄的牆紙。

Great Pride and Meanness sure are near ally'd; Or thin Partitions do their Bounds divide.

1753年

兩隻會聽話的耳朵，勝過一百張會說話的嘴巴。

A Pair of good Ears will drain dry an hundred Tongues.

敬愛的讀者：

這是我第二十次透過這種方法與您溝通，人們一直以來很支持我的創作，對此我深感榮幸。最讓我開心的是，我對於天氣的預報讓人們很滿意。千真萬確，我的預報都要經過認真的計算之後才可以做出。甚至，我敢大聲說，我預測的天氣，在我們這個微小的行星上，無論哪個角落，我預言的風雨霜雪都會如期而至（因為我們觀測的行星距離地球幾千英里，所以我想這樣的準確度，您也是可以接受的）；在其他方面，我可以保證適用的曆書範圍是在北方殖民地範圍之內。至於最重要的天氣，這個問題因為備受關注，所以我決定擴大它的應用範圍，將南北半球囊括進來，其最終版圖從哈德遜灣延伸至合恩角的廣大區域。

這本曆書依然使用我此前的方式進行呈現，這樣才可以符合議會法案中的最新條款，關於這一點，我已經在去年的曆書中提過。新的條款對第一項條款進行修訂，但是對我們沒有本質上的影響，它的最終目的只是為了規範一些英國的商業活動。所以，我們的變動僅限於：在每個月的第二頁添加一欄，用來進行新舊版本的對照，我想這應該是可行的。好吧，前言先寫到這裡（我相信您也不希望看到太長的前言，而是希望把足夠的空間留給更實用的內容）。

您的朋友以及僕人，

理查・桑德斯

支付利息會違背某些人的原則，支付本金卻會傷害另一些人的利益。

'Tis against some Men's Principle to pay Interest, and seems against other's Interest to pay the Principal.

哲學家和紈絝子弟經常改變時尚。

Philosophy as well as Foppery often changes Fashion.

樹立太過美好的榜樣，其實是一種很難被原諒的詆毀行為，是所謂「詆毀權貴」的行為。（譯者注：Scandalum Magnatum，英國舊語，意為詆毀權貴）

Setting too good an Example is a Kind of Slander seldom forgiven; 'tis Scandalum Magnatum.

喜歡說話的人不一定是傻子，但是信任他的人一定是真蠢。

A great Talker may be no Fool, but he is one that relies on him.

理性開口教導人們的時候，你如果不聽，她就會往你的耳朵上招呼一拳。

When Reason preaches, if you won't hear her she'll box your Ears.

空閒時間如果沒有被妥善利用，就不是真正的空閒。

It is not Leisure that is not used.

統治者如果無法有效作為，老百姓的善意就無法被激發出來。

The Good-will of the Governed will be starv'd, if not fed by the good Deeds of the Governors.

遇上繪畫和打架，最好站在遠處觀望，不可近前摻和。

Paintings and Fightings are best seen at a distance.

如果想要獲得稱讚，你必須撒下種子——言行舉止要溫文爾雅。

If you would reap Praise you must sow the Seeds, gentle Words and useful Deeds.

愚昧無知讓人拉幫結派，羞愧恥辱讓人泥足深陷。

Ignorance leads Men into a Party, and Shame keeps them from getting out again.

欲速則不達，忙中多出錯。

Haste makes Waste.

突然得來的權力容易讓人狂傲無禮，突如其來的自由容易讓人舉止粗俗；但是良好的舉止需要一點一點地累積習得。

Sudden Power is apt to be insolent, Sudden Liberty saucy; that behaves best which has grown gradually.

最瞭解這個世界的人，最不喜歡這個世界。

He that best understands the World, least likes it.

生氣總是有原因，但是這個原因很少有理。

Anger is never without a Reason, but seldom with a good One.

認為金錢無所不能的人，很可能只會一心為錢，罔顧其他。

He that is of Opinion Money will do every Thing, may well be suspected of doing every Thing for Money.

惡化的傷口可以復原，壞名聲卻很難挽回。

An ill Wound, but not an ill Name, may be healed.

一朝失勢無人識，一朝得勢不識己。

When out of Favour, none know thee; when in, thou dost not know thyself.

一份薄獎勝過大肆稱讚。

A lean Award is better than a fat Judgment.

上帝、父母、師長的恩情，永遠報不完。

God, Parents, and Instructors, can never be requited.

蓋房之前不計算成本，是愚蠢的行為；計算成本之後才蓋房，又會發現自己估計失誤。

He that builds before he counts the Cost, acts foolishly; and he that counts before he builds, finds he did not count wisely.

做交易有耐心，每年都可以獲利。

Patience in Market, is worth Pounds in a Year.

危險只是祈禱的調味品——人們總是面臨危險的時候，才會想到要祈禱。

Danger is Sauce for Prayers.

罐裡沒蜂蜜，嘴上卻要甜——嘴要甜，會說話。

If you have no Honey in your Pot, have some in your Mouth.

兩隻會聽話的耳朵，勝過一百張會說話的嘴巴。

A Pair of good Ears will drain dry an hundred Tongues.

如果想要出人頭地，沒有什麼比空有滿腔抱負更低微的。

Nothing humbler than Ambition, when it is about to climb.

不知滿足的人找不到安樂椅。

The discontented Man finds no easy Chair.

心懷美德跟身懷一技是留給孩子最好的財富。

Virtue and a Trade, are a Child's best Portion.

最想要的禮物是有償的，不是白給的。

Gifts much expected, are paid, not given.

1754年

柳條雖弱，卻可以綁住柴火。

Willows arc weak, but they bind the Faggot.

善良的讀者：

到目前為止，我為您效勞的時間已經可以帶出三批學徒了，儘管我現在年事已高，卻從來沒有想過停止為您服務；但是如果我可以用帶出三批學徒還多三倍的時間為您效力，我應該是非常高興的。我想，第一個星象學家一定是一個非常老實的農民，而且似乎最後一個也會是農民。因為我的兄弟傑曼和摩爾，以及我自己是這個國家僅存的曆書作家，我們也同屬農民階級。儘管我中途到了大城市拜師學藝，甚至到過宮廷、見過皇帝，也見證從巴比倫國王尼布甲尼撒一世到英國女王詹姆斯一世的所有歷史，但是你可能會問，你要怎樣才可以證明第一個星象學家是農民？我認為這件事情不在歷史的記錄裡，因為星象學出現的時間比文字更早，但我還是從天空這本包羅萬象的書中，從十二星座的名稱中找到答案。為什麼？因為這些星座的名稱在很大程度上與農務有關，用來描述一年之中連在一起的幾個月，同時透過這種方式來滿足人們對曆書的需求。因為古代的一年是從春季開始算起，這樣看來，白羊座和金牛座，也就是公羊座和公牛座，代表的是羊群和牛群會在星座所屬的季節裡大量繁殖。雙子座最初是「孩子」的意思，但是後來改為雙胞胎，是因為山羊一般都是一次生下兩隻小羊。接著是巨蟹座，也就是螃蟹這種像魚的生物當季的時候。再接下來是獅子座，獅子和處女，或是少女座，代表的是夏季的月份和三伏酷暑期，也是草原上的獅子活動頻繁而少女精力旺盛的時節。秋天最先到來的是天秤座，天秤座代表平衡，表示收割、稱量、售賣盛夏果實的時候到了，或是也可以說是閒暇時節到了，有趣的是，這個時候往往是人們忙著跟自己的鄰里打官司上法庭的時節。我知道有些人認為這個星座應該代表晝夜平分的時刻到了，但是實際上，接下來的這個星座——天蠍座，更具有這樣的含義。天蠍座，顧名思義，就是指一隻坐在自己尾巴上的蠍子，也暗示支付費用的意思。再接下來是射手座，也就是人馬座，說明狩獵的時候到了；因為這個時節的樹木和灌木叢已經葉落歸根，所以人們更容易看見獵物，射中獵物。山羊（譯者注：疑為筆誤，應該是摩羯座）與晝短夜長的冬天相攜而過，這是一個充滿歡笑和盛宴的季節，因為摩羯座意味著跳舞或是跳躍。然後我們的水瓶座終於到了，她也被稱為寶瓶座，展示的是雨雪紛飛、洪流肆虐的季節；最後是雙魚座，或是叫做兩條鮭魚座，意思是那些魚兒會沿岸游回河流上游：請準備好你的衣服，補好你的漁網，把它們抓來醃漬起來。朋友們，這就是一盤上好的下酒菜，配著窖藏的蘋果酒正好。但是如果你抓不到鮭魚，抓到鯖魚也很不錯。我知道，善解人意的讀者們，你們之中有很多人都期待可以看到一篇序言，但是如果無法如願，你們就會覺得自己被怠慢。所以現在的這篇文字，或多或少可以讓你們滿意。儘管它祈禱的作用可能不大，但是如今很多曆書更不值得讀了。

所以，您看，我已經在朋友們的檢驗下刪掉很多常見的內容，否則這本書會更厚更大。但是，在您看來，也許這個厚度的「良心」書籍已經可以滿足所有的讀者當下的需要，當然我也是這麼想的。

愛您，願為您效勞的朋友，

理查・桑德斯

天下第一等傻事是自以為是，自作聰明；其次是自以為是還要到處誇口；第三是蔑視別人給的忠告。

The first Degree of Folly, is to conceit one's self wise; the second to profess it; the third to despise Counsel.

當心再甜的酒也會變酸，脾氣再好的人也會生氣。

Take heed of the Vinegar of sweet Wine, and the Anger of Good-nature.

鐘聲敲響，提醒人們上教堂，但是它自己從來不關心布道說了什麼。

The Bell calls others to Church, but itself never minds the Sermon.

砍斷母雞的翅膀、希望的雙翼，以免你被它們帶著到處跑。

Cut the Wings of your Hens and Hopes, lest they lead you a weary Dance after them.

最輕的東西浮在河面上，最沒有才華的人卻站在不好的政府權力的頂端。

In Rivers & bad Governments, the lightest Things swim at top.

貓戴著手套抓不到老鼠。

The Cat in Gloves catches no Mice.

如果想要知道錢的分量，就去向別人借一些。

If you'd know the Value of Money, go and borrow some.

馬兒想的是一回事，馬鞍上的人想的又是另一回事。

The Horse thinks one thing, and he that saddles him another.

愛你的鄰居，但是不要拆掉隔斷的籬笆。

Love your Neighbour; yet don't pull down your Hedge.

成功順利地登上馬背，就放開手中的韁繩，很快她就會從馬鞍上摔下來。

When Prosperity was well mounted, she let go the Bridle, and soon came tumbling out of the Saddle.

有些人因為良心作祟，上教堂戴帽子，但是劫掠聖壇的時候卻忘記良心這回事。

Some make Conscience of wearing a Hat in the Church, who make none of robbing the Altar.

友誼若想長青，不需客套虛禮，禮貌卻不能少。

Friendship cannot live with Ceremony, nor without Civility.

少表揚，少貶低，褒貶要適宜。

Praise little, dispraise less.

有學問的傻子比沒學問的笨蛋更能說善道，儘管如此，說的還是一些廢話。

The learned Fool writes his Nonsense in better Language than the unlearned; but still 'tis Nonsense.

孩子心裡的20先令跟20年是永遠花不完的。

A Child thinks 20 Shillings and 20 Years can scarce ever be spent.

不要總是想著自己的精明而忘記別人也同樣精明：1.5個精明人就是完勝單槍匹馬的1個精明人。

Don't think so much of your own Cunning, as to forget other Men's: A cunning Man is overmatch'd by a cunning Man and a Half.

柳條雖弱，卻可以綁住柴火。

Willows are weak, but they bind the Faggot.

你可以給人加官晉爵，卻無法給他決斷能力。

You may give a Man an Office, but you cannot give him Discretion.

做了不應該做的事情，就會有不想要的感覺。（譯者注：做了虧心事，半夜就怕鬼敲門。昧著良心做事，會遭到良心的譴責。）

He that doth what he should not, shall feel what he would not.

跟愚蠢的朋友關係親密，就像睡在剃刀上。

To be intimate with a foolish Friend, is like going to bed to a Razor.

小無賴容易變成大流氓。（譯者注：小錯不改，鑄成大錯）

Little Rogues easily become great Ones.

有時候，你的自我感覺會很棒；有時候，又會覺得自己一無是處。

You may sometimes be much in the wrong, in owning your being in the right.

朋友才是王子真正的權杖。

Friends are the true Sceptres of Princes.

沒有理性的地方，什麼都匱乏。

Where Sense is wanting, every thing is wanting.

自古以來，有很多王子跟大衛王一樣，都是有罪的，但是很少有人像大衛王那樣懺悔。

Many Princes sin with David, but few repent with him.

運氣不好不壞，一心祈求好運。

He that hath no ill Fortune will be troubled with good.

為了年老和急需，有時候要節省：早晨的太陽不會一直掛到晚上。

For Age and Want save while you may; No Morning Sun lasts a whole Day.

知識之於好學者，就如財富之於細心者，權力之於膽大者，天堂之於有德者。

Learning to the Studious; Riches to the Careful; Power to the Bold; Heaven to the Virtuous.

現在，請用聖誕的歡呼帶給窮苦人歡樂吧；
感謝上帝，是你的大能讓這一年結束。
Now glad the Poor with Christmas Cheer;
Thank God you're able so to end the Year.

1755年

你若想被愛，先要愛人，也要可愛。

If you would be loved, love and be loveable.

尊敬的讀者：

俗話說，世界上有一半的人不瞭解另一半的人的生活。所以，為了給您補充一些這個方面的相關知識，我已經在之前的一本曆書中為您介紹哈德遜海灣人們的生活方式，以及因為極致酷寒的天氣狀況而造成的影響。雖然所有這些都是千真萬確的，但是很有可能讓一些讀者感到奇怪，甚至將看到的內容視作虛構小說裡的情節。在這本曆書中，我會為您帶來一些與熱帶國家相關的資訊，讓您瞭解熱帶地區的天氣變化是極為顯著的（因為人們總是自然地認為熱帶地區的景觀都是相同的模樣）。

這份報告是從布格先生的日記裡摘錄下來的，布格先生是一位法國學者，曾經在國王的指派下，測量等分線下的一處緯度，以便幫助解決英、法兩國哲學家針對地球形狀產生的爭論。與此同時，也有一些人出於同樣的目的，被指派到北極圈的拉普蘭進行測量。那個國家的山很高，相比之下，我們國家的山只是一些矮小的鼴鼠山。這份摘錄主要描寫的是那些高聳入雲的山脈。

今年曆書的寫法與往年的一致，唯一的不同是：我會將一些主要恆星的名字放在曆書的第三欄上。此外，我還會標示這些恆星在晚上九點到達子午線的日期，讓對這些知識不熟悉的人有機會進行瞭解。

我是隨時感激您的朋友和僕人，

理查・桑德斯

一個男人沒有老婆，只能算是半個男人。（譯者注：沒有妻子的男人不完整）

A Man without a Wife, is but half a Man.

話要少說，事要多做。

Speak little, do much.

經常出遊的人要少吃。

He that would travel much, should eat little.

紅酒喝下肚，真話說出來。（譯者注：酒後吐真言）

When the Wine enters, out goes the Truth.

你若想被愛，先要愛人，也要可愛。

If you would be loved, love and be loveable.

求來的擁有，有時候要價也很貴。

Ask and have, is sometimes dear buying.

母狗心一急，生出盲狗崽。

The hasty Bitch brings forth blind Puppies.

餓殍滿地，有法無效；有法不守，飢餓降臨。

Where there is Hunger, Law is not regarded; and where Law is not regarded, there will be Hunger.

兩根乾柴火點燃一根綠樹枝。

Two dry Sticks will burn a green One.

誠實的人先苦後甜，不誠實的人先甜後苦。

The honest Man takes Pains, and then enjoys Pleasures; the Knave takes Pleasure, and then suffers Pains.

人生有三件事情需要考慮：第一件，你從哪裡來；第二件，要到哪裡去；第三件，你需要向誰交代。

Think of three Things: whence you came, where you are going, and to whom you must account.

劣質鋼做不出精品刀。

There was never a good Knife made of bad Steel.

狼皮每年換一次，狼性從來改不了。

The Wolf sheds his Coat once a Year, his Disposition never.

誰聰明？以人為師的人。（譯者注：善於向別人學習的人）

誰強大？可以妥善管理自己激情的人。

誰富有？知足的人。

這個人到底是誰？沒有人。（譯者注：沒有人可以做到）

Who is wise? He that learns from every One.

Who is powerful? He that governs his Passions.

Who is rich? He that is content.

Who is that? Nobody.

肚飽惡念生。

A full Belly brings forth every Evil.

時間短，任務重，工人懶，酬勞高，老闆催；懶骨頭，快起來，時間不等人，工作要完成。

The Day is short, the Work great, the Workmen lazy, the Wages high, the Master urgeth; Up, then, and be doing.

智慧之門從未關閉。

The Doors of Wisdom are never shut.

藥草價值多，人類美德少。

Much Virtue in Herbs, little in Men.

主人幹活，用眼多，用手少。

The Master's Eye will do more Work than both his Hands.

嘗甜憶苦。（譯者注：嘴裡嘗著蜂蜜，心中想著苦膽——居安思危）

When you taste Honey, remember Gall.

無知並不可恥，可恥的是無心向學。

Being ignorant is not so much a Shame, as being unwilling to learn.

上帝把所有的東西都賜給勤奮。（譯者注：勤奮的人受到上帝的眷顧）

God gives all Things to Industry.

即使有一百個小偷，也難從渾身赤裸的人身上撈到好處，尤其是這個人已經窮得脫了一層皮。

An hundred Thieves cannot strip one naked Man, especially if his Skin's off.

勤奮戰勝困難，懶惰製造困難。

Diligence overcomes Difficulties, Sloth makes them.

小錯不改，大禍臨頭。

Neglect mending a small Fault, and 'twill soon be a great One.

不良的受益等於真正的損失。

Bad Gains are truly Losses.

長命百歲也許還不夠美好，美好的生命卻是長命百歲的。

A long Life may not be good enough, but a good Life is long enough.

跟你的惡習抗爭到底，跟你的鄰居和睦相處，讓你每個新年都越來越好——更上一層樓。

Be at War with your Vices, at Peace with your Neighbours, and let every New-Year find you a better Man.

1756年

愛你的敵人，因為他們對你的過錯總是直言不諱。

Love your Enemies, for they tell you your Faults.

敬愛的讀者：

儘管您在我的曆書裡查看到的內容大多是每個月的日子、重大的日期、月亮的變化、太陽和月亮的升起落下，並且由此預知潮漲潮落和天氣變化這類的資訊，除此之外，似乎沒有其他價值，但我還是願意相信您買書的這筆錢花得很值得。

此外，出於實用性和娛樂性的考慮，每年我都會再為您準備其他的天文逸事，以滿足您的需求，現在正好是介紹土星兩次公轉的好時機。但是，我希望您收穫的不止於我說的這些，所以我充分地利用曆書的空白處，插入許多道德格言、智慧箴言、節儉座右銘，就是為了將誠實、理性、勤奮、節儉的好處深深地刻進讀者的認知裡。如果您有留意到並且親身實踐，很有可能您現在已經變得更有智慧也更加富有，所以您收穫到價值已經數倍於買書所花的錢。

但是請放心，我的曆書不會因為您變得富有而趁機漲價，相反地，為了感謝您一直以來的大力支持，我還在曆書裡加入一些有益心智以及身體健康的「秘方」，並且經過專人實踐，證明有效。祝願意相信並且準備實踐的讀者您幸福快樂。

永遠心懷感激的朋友，

理查・桑德斯

命運的沉浮不會對一個有智慧的人造成傷害，正如月亮的圓缺對他沒有什麼影響一般。

A Change of Fortune hurts a wise Man no more than a Change of the Moon.

即使傷害、過失、爭端使你不快樂，也請相信你會重新振作，上天自有安排。

Does Mischief, Misconduct, & Warrings displease ye; Think there's a Providence, 'twill make ye easy.

我的勝過我們的。

Mine is better than Ours.

愛你的敵人，因為他們對你的過錯總是直言不諱。

Love your Enemies, for they tell you your Faults.

身懷一技的人，名利雙收皆有望。

He that has a Trade, has an Office of Profit and Honour.

禮貌對待每個人，適時幫助許多人，用心熟悉一些人，真心結交一個人。以上這些，如能做到，若問敵人，一個沒有。

Be civil to all; serviceable to many; familiar with few;

Friend to one; Enemy to none.

虛榮可以開花，卻無法結果。

Vain-Glory flowereth, but beareth no Fruit.

刑法太輕，少有人遵守；律例過嚴，難以被施行。

Laws too gentle are seldom obeyed; too severe, seldom executed.

無所事事，心生煩憂；安逸舒適，艱辛來到。

Trouble springs from Idleness; Toil from Ease.

去愛，還要被愛。

Love, and be loved.

智者不會只是一味地追求，只依靠正義手段得到應該獲得的，頭腦清醒地利用已有的，心懷歡喜地分配出去，最後心滿意足地離開。

A wise Man will desire no more, than what he may get justly, use soberly, distribute chearfully, and leave contentedly.

勤快的紡車轉得快，紡得多。

The diligent Spinner has a large Shift.

假朋友就像影子，太陽照在你的身上就會出來。

A false Friend and a Shadow, attend only while the Sun shines.

明天，每個錯誤都可以改正過來，但是那樣的明天永遠不會到來。

Tomorrow, every Fault is to be amended; but that Tomorrow never comes.

懶漢沉睡你深耕，打下糧食，要賣要儲，你來決定。

Plough deep, while Sluggards sleep; and you shall have Corn, to sell and to keep.

播種荊棘的人，最好不要光著腳走路。

He that sows Thorns, should never go barefoot.

懶散走得實在慢，貧窮不久就趕上。

Laziness travels so slowly, that Poverty soon overtakes him.

力士參孫，四肢發達，頭腦簡單，否則不會沉溺在妓女的溫柔鄉。

Sampson with his strong Body, had a weak Head, or he would not have laid it in a Harlot's Lap.

朋友跟朋友做生意，也要明碼標價，仔細算帳。只有這樣，友誼才可以天長地久。（譯者注：親兄弟也要明算帳）

When a Friend deals with a Friend, let the Bargain be clear and well penn'd, that they may continue Friends to the End.

從來不多吃的人，也從來不偷懶。

He that never eats too much, will never be lazy.

因為有知識而自豪，就像被光亮弄瞎眼；因為有美德而自傲，就像用解藥毒自己。

To be proud of Knowledge, is to be blind with Light; to be proud of Virtue, is to poison yourself with the Antidote.

賺你可以賺的，賺到就要守住，這才是讓你點石成金的點金石。

Get what you can, and what you get, hold; 'Tis the Stone that will turn all your Lead into Gold.

不是自己應得的錢財或稱讚，一個真正的人是不會接受的。（譯者注：無功不受祿）

An honest Man will receive neither Money nor Praise, that is not his Due.

說跟做，彼此之間吵了架，分了家。

Saying and Doing, have quarrel'd and parted.

請指出我的過錯，也請改正你自己的錯誤。

Tell me my Faults, and mend your own.

1757年

抱著可以活一百年的心態去工作，懷著明天就會死去的心態去祈禱。

Work as if you were to live 100 Years, Pray as if you were to die Tomorrow.

敬愛的讀者：

對於我們人類來說，任何世俗的擔憂都比不上健康重要。我們每時每刻的呼吸，以及選擇一個健康的居住環境，這兩者在很大程度上決定我們的健康。這些都是非常重要的事情，值得每個初涉世事的市民深思熟慮。尤其因為這不僅在很大程度上關係到生活的舒適度，其本身更是生活的必備條件。如果一個家庭經常有人生病，這個家庭很難興盛起來。以下的內容是我從普林格爾——一位醫學博士近期發表的文章中摘錄的，關於這個主題，我希望可以被讀者接受，也可以幫助到其中一些人。

我聽說有些人已經開始他們的偉大冒險——嘗試飼養去年我在曆書中推薦的公牛。對我而言，可以跟人們交流實用的技巧是一件樂事，也是我服務人們的一種途徑。有些人偶爾寫信把他們的觀察體會告訴我，如果有可能，這些想法還會出現在我下一本曆書中，我也因此十分感激，感激他們讓我體驗到如此多的快樂。

您忠誠的朋友，

理查・桑德斯

想要在宮廷加官晉爵，就要先趴在地上，匍匐前進。

He that would rise at Court, must begin by Creeping.

很多人心裡想一套，嘴上說一套。

Many a Man's own Tongue gives Evidence against his Understanding.

眼淚流過就乾，乾得最快。

Nothing dries sooner than a Tear.

建造兩個煙囪比讓一個煙囪經常冒煙更容易。

'Tis easier to build two Chimneys, than maintain one in Fuel.

小怒無傷大雅，大怒傷身費神。

Anger warms the Invention, but overheats the Oven.

叫傻瓜沉默不算有禮貌，讓他接著說卻也殘忍。

It is Ill-Manners to silence a Fool, and Cruelty to let him go on.

紅綢布、天鵝絨，送主婦，可滅火。

Scarlet, Silk and Velvet, have put out the Kitchen Fire.

想要抓到魚，就要捨得魚餌。

He that would catch Fish, must venture his Bait.

人們因為錯誤需要花費的心思，比彌補錯誤花費得更多。

Men take more pains to mask than mend.

兩個明天抵不過一個今天。

One Today is worth two Tomorrows.

人若真心誠意，魅力難以抗拒，遇見凶殘敵手，亦能迫其繳械：心中坦蕩無算計，外在赤裸無掩飾，心思單純，想法簡單，不識拐彎抹角，只會全然表達：錯誤之形被她帶走，美德之神因她存在。善良源頭，光芒萬丈！降臨身邊，助我成長，護我心靈，察我言行。

Sincerity has such resistless Charms, she oft the fiercest of our Foes disarms: No Art she knows, in native Whiteness dress'd, her Thoughts all pure, and therefore all express'd: She takes from Error its Deformity; and without her all other Virtues die. Bright Source of Goodness! to my Aid descend, watch o'er my Heart, and all my Words attend.

所謂安全的方法，其實從來都不安全。

The way to be safe, is never to be secure.

不要跟別人的女人調情，不要垂涎別人的財產。

Dally not with other Folks' Women or Money.

抱著可以活一百年的心態去工作，懷著明天就會死去的心態去祈禱。

Work as if you were to live 100 Years, Pray as if you were to die Tomorrow.

聰明過了頭，反被聰明騙：

開玩笑，要留心，有人聽了笑一笑，有人聽後會計較。

人們善於偽裝，臉上和顏悅色，心中恨意滔天。看著雲淡風輕，實際痛苦萬分。

我們真是大錯特錯，一心以為痛會自癒，

嗚呼哀哉！如此行徑，只會讓結果適得其反。

如斯痛苦，正如指甲抓傷口——痛上加痛，

即使時間流逝，只會加深潰爛，徒增痛苦。

Excess of Wit may oftentimes beguile:

Jests are not always pardon'd ——by a Smile.

Men may disguise their Malice at the Heart, and seem at Ease ——tho' pain'd with inward Smart.

Mistaken, we ——think all such Wounds of course reflection cures; ——alas! it makes them worse.

Like Scratches they with double Anguish seize, Rankle in time, and fester by Degrees.

就像一位端莊典雅的貴夫人，

信仰閃耀著極致美好的光輝，

理智在此刻教導我們要尊重這位夫人，

絕對不能說輕浮的笑話，敗壞她的名聲。

日常生活中，你也要明白這個道理，

除了傻瓜，沒有人總是濫開俗氣的玩笑，

從現在開始，就不要再犯傻了，

也不要認為小心無用，

因為只有禮貌恭敬的人，

才不必擔心不敬神。

Like some grave Matron of a noble Line,

With awful Beauty does Religion shine.

Just Sense should teach us to revere the Dame,
Nor, by imprudent Jests, to spot her Fame.
In common Life you'll own this Reas'ning right,
That none but Fools in gross Abuse delight:
Then use it here ——nor think the Caution vain;
To be polite, Men need not be profane.

自以為是的人把豐盛當作早餐，貧窮當作正餐，壞名聲當作晚餐。

Pride breakfasted with Plenty, dined with Poverty, supped with Infamy.

退隱無法總是可以擔保美德：很多人在都市裡表現正直，卻在山野間顯出邪惡。

Retirement does not always secure Virtue; Lot was upright in the City, wicked in the Mountain.

遊手好閒是一片死海，吞沒所有的美德：所以，請在工作中表現積極，這樣一來，誘惑為你設下的陷阱就會落空：不飛的鳥兒容易被射中。

Idleness is the Dead Sea, that swallows all Virtues: Be active in Business, that Temptation may miss her Aim: The Bird that sits, is easily shot.

恥辱和腹痛是上一代人的疾病，現在似乎已經被治癒。

Shame and the Dry-belly-ach were Diseases of the last Age; this seems to be cured of them.

為了生計去念法律或物理，或是其他文理科目，儘管開始的時候你會感覺困難重重，心生厭倦，這個時候你需要拿出耐心和毅力，奮發進取；慢慢的，學習任務的乏味之感會與日消散，你的辛勞終將贏來成功的冠冕。這樣一來，你會超越所有在學業上粗心大意、懶惰散漫、思慮淺薄的對手，並且成為專業翹楚。能力掌控事業，事業掌控財富，到了一定的年紀，財富就可以為你提供輕鬆又體面的退休條件。

In studying Law or Physick, or any other Art or Science, by which you propose to get your Livelihood, though you find it at first hard, difficult and unpleasing, use Diligence, Patience and Perseverance; the Irksomness of your Task will thus diminish daily, and your Labour shall finally be crowned with Success. You shall go beyond all your Competitors who are careless, idle or superficial in their Acquisitions, and be at the Head of your Profession. —— Ability will command Business, Business Wealth; and Wealth an easy and honourable Retirement when Age shall require it.

靠近西班牙漫長海岸線的地方，幾座小島依然矗立在驚濤之中；歌聲婉轉的詩人說，那裡住著古老的民族，他們個個都是彈無虛發的投擲者，出生以後，尚在襁褓，他們脆弱的神經就要忍受考驗；沒有制勝的技藝，就沒有飽腹的食物。標準定下，年少者經常失敗，努力皆廢，一無所獲的痛苦隨著不辨方向的石頭飛轉：

長期操練帶來完美技藝，之前讓他們深感挫敗的任務，如今不過小菜一碟，鵝卵石自手臂處疾速飛出，一擊即中，石塊飛向高空，獵取撲騰翅膀的犧牲品。故而，人類的所有技藝都需要循序漸進，才可以臻於完美，數月的辛苦換來經年的舒服。

Near to the wide extended Coasts of Spain, some Islands triumph o'er the raging Main; Where dwelt of old, as tuneful Poets say, Slingers, who bore from all the Prize away. While Infants yet, their feeble Nerves they try'd; Nor needful Food, till won by Art, supply'd. Fix'd was the Mark, the Youngster oft in vain, whirl'd the misguided Stone with fruitless Pain:

'Till, by long Practice, to Perfection brought, with easy Sleight their former

Task they wrought. Swift from their Arm th' unerring Pebble flew, and high in Air, the flutt'ring Victim slew. So in each Art Men rise but by Degrees, and Months of Labour lead to Years of Ease.

儘管獒犬生性溫和，咬人也是要動牙齒的。

Tho' the Mastiff be gentle, yet bite him not by the Lip.

大方施予不會降低人們的生活水準。

Great-Alms-giving, lessens no Man's Living.

王冠治不好頭疼。

The royal Crown cures not the Head-ach.

為人處事正直不欺，流言蜚語不放心裡；爛泥黏得在土牆上，卻無法掩蓋大理石的光輝。

Act uprightly, and despise Calumny; Dirt may stick to a Mud Wall, but not to polish'd Marble.

借錢的人是放貸人的奴隸，擔保人卻同時是這二者的奴隸。

The Borrower is a Slave to the Lender; the Security to both.

離經叛道卻自以為是毀掉了很多人：堅信大眾的看法，才是快樂之所在。

Singularity in the right, hath ruined many: Happy those who are convinced of the general Opinion.

舌頭冒犯人，耳朵遭掌摑。

The Tongue offends, and the Ears get the Cuffing.

一些古代哲學家說，幸福更多依靠心靈的內在性格而非外部環境；在任何場合都不覺得幸福的人，永遠與幸福無緣。

他們告訴我們，想要幸福，就要知足。這句話說得對，但是他們沒有教導我們如何才可以知足。窮理查將要給你一條短小實用的準則。想要感到滿足，回頭看看那些不如你的人，不要向前看那些比你富足的人。如果這樣仍然無法使你知足，你就不配得到幸福。

Some antient Philosophers have said, that Happiness depends more on the inward Disposition of Mind than on outward Circumstances; and that he who cannot be happy in any State, can be so in no State.

To be happy, they tell us we must be content. Right. But they do not teach how we may become content. Poor Richard shall give you a short good Rule for that. To be content, look backward on those who possess less than yourself, not forward on those who possess more. If this does not make you content, you don't deserve to be happy.

學識是生命中一件相當寶貴的財富，但是虔誠的重要性更無可比擬，因為它可以讓我們幸福，無論是現在還是將來。在審判之日，沒有人會問我們多麼精通語言或是哲學，但是會問我們是否在教義規定的指引下，善良虔誠地度過這一生，這是因為人們生來就被賦予理性。在那一刻，我們曾經給渺小的螞蟻巢穴扔下一把麵粉或穀殼的善行，比我們可以召集日月星辰或是可以正確說出每顆星星的名字，對我們更有益處。因為到了那個時候，群星自身將會消失，太陽和月亮也將光輝不再，自然界的構造都會毀滅。但是我們做的好事或壞事一直存留，記載在永恆的文件中。

Learning is a valuable Thing in the Affairs of this Life, but of infinitely more Importance is Godliness, as it tends not only to make us happy here but hereafter. At the Day of Judgment, we shall not be asked, what Proficiency we have made in Languages or Philosophy; but whether we have liv'd virtuously and piously, as Men endued with Reason, guided by the Dictates of Religion. In that Hour it will more avail us, that we have thrown a Handful of Flour or Chaff in Charity to a Nest of contemptible Pismires, than that we could muster all the Hosts of Heaven, and call every Star by its proper Name. For then the Constellations themselves shall disappear, the Sun and Moon shall give no more Light, and all the Frame of Nature shall vanish. But our good or bad Works shall remain for ever, recorded in the Archives of Eternity.

不吃晚飯去睡覺，一身無債醒過來。

Sleep without Supping, and you'll rise without owing for it.

其他罪行隨著年月老去，貪婪卻始終風華正茂，聖誕節也要送食物給窮人。

When other Sins grow old by Time, then Avarice is in its prime, yet feed the Poor at Christmas time.

有德者們不動聲色地現身了，在他們淡漠的表情下，卻穿著冷靜安心的外衣（譯者注：有安撫人心的力量）。他們自東西面、南北境來，從最正義的法官手中拿走自己的命運（譯者注：描寫的是末日審判的情景，故此可以看作聽取命運的審判）；這個人正在安詳地注視著他們（他的面前放著生命之書，所有的秘密一覽無遺）；「按照你的工作，你得到賞賜：讓你得到不死的王國，早已為你備好永恆的約定。」

Unmov'd alone the Virtuous now appear, and in their Looks a calm Assurance wear. From East, from West, from North and South they come, to take from the most righteous Judge their Doom; Who thus, to them, with a serene Regard; (The Books of Life before him laid, And all the secret Records wide display'd) "According to your Works be your Reward: Possess immortal Kingdoms as your Due, prepar'd from an eternal Date for you."

1758年

沉默寡言不總是象徵智慧，喋喋不休卻總是代表愚蠢。

Silence is not always a Sign of Wisdom, but Babbling is ever a Mark of Folly.

敬愛的讀者：

我曾經聽別人說，作為一名作家，人生最大的幸事莫過於讓同為作家的博學者滿懷崇敬之情地引用自己的作品。只是我很少體驗到這種喜悅，因為儘管我到今年為止已經連續出版二十五本曆書，佔了一個世紀四分之一的時間，怎麼說也算得上一個知名曆書作家，但是不知道為什麼，本來應該與我「親如手足」的同行們卻很少送給我喝采的歡呼和鼓勵的掌聲，很少有人會把注意力稍微移到我的身上。所以我只能說，寫作沒有為我帶來實實在在的「布丁」——物質上的豐富，無人讚賞的窘境也讓我倍感失落。

我最終得出結論，只有花錢買書的讀者們才是評判我價值的「裁判」。此外，有時候漫步在沒有人認識我的地方，我經常可以聽到一兩個人引用我曆書裡的諺語，他們都會在最後一句加上「正如窮理查所說」，這給我帶來極大的滿足。因為這不僅表示我的規諫受到人們的重視，也表示我在一些人的心中具有權威性。對於我個人而言，為了督促自己牢記以及重複那些智慧的話語，我有時候也會很認真地自我引用。

現在，我的「裁判」，我講述一件事情給您聽，讓您看看我有多麼滿足。有一次，我騎馬經過一個熙熙攘攘的市集，人們聚集在一起等著商品拍賣開始，我也停下馬來準備湊個熱鬧。當時還沒有到拍賣時間，圍觀的人們彼此在聊天，感慨世道的艱難。其中有一個人對旁邊一位白髮蒼蒼、衣著樸素卻整潔的老人說：「我向您祈禱，亞伯拉罕神父。您怎麼看當今這個世道？難道沉重的賦稅不會毀掉這個國家嗎？我們怎麼可能負擔得起這麼沉重的賦稅？對此，您有什麼高見嗎？」亞伯拉罕神父站起來回答：「儘管你很想要我的建議，但是我可以給你的卻不多。因為『智者一句話就足夠了，說太多反而填不滿一蒲式耳（譯者注：有智慧的人往往一語中的，話太多的不一定可以解決問題），正如窮理查所說。』」周圍的人全部聚攏，看著他，希望他闡述自己的想法。於是，他接著說出以下這些話：

「各位朋友，」他說，「各位街坊，現在的賦稅確實很沉重，如果我們只是支付政府強制徵收的那個部分，其實還容易應付。但是實際上，還有很多其他的稅等著我們繳納，我們其中的一些人就會無法承受。我們會因為遊手好閒而需要繳納雙倍的賦稅，因為驕傲自大而需要繳納三倍的賦稅，因為自身愚昧而需要繳納四倍的賦稅，對於這些類型的賦稅，就連徵稅官也無法幫助我們減免分毫。然而，我們還是傾聽一些規諫吧，這樣可能多少會對我們有些幫助。正如窮理查在1733年的曆書裡說：『天助自助者』。」

「人們心目中的『硬政府』——嚴苛的政府向民眾徵收的稅，需要民眾貢獻十分之一的工作時間才可以賺到。但是如果我們可以想想那些所有花在懶惰或是無所事事上的時間，那些被用去做無聊的事情或是娛樂的時光，我們就會發現，相比之下，無所事事對我們徵收的稅更多。懶惰帶來疾病，當然也會削減壽命。正如窮理查所說，懶惰如鐵鏽，侵蝕甚於鑄就；常用的鑰匙磨得亮。窮理查還說，如果你熱愛生命，就不要揮霍時間，因為生命正是由時間構成的。」

「我們花費太多不必要的時間在睡覺上啊！完全不記得窮理查說過的『睡著的狐狸抓不到雞禽』，也忘記『死後自會長眠地下』的告誡。如果時間是最珍貴的東西，用窮理查的話來說，『浪費時間，就是極大的揮霍與糟蹋』。因為，他曾經在其他地方告誡我們：『失去的時間難找回；我們總是說時間夠用，其實時間根本不夠用。』所以，讓我們起床來做事吧，我們要做的是有意義的事情；這樣一來，辛勤勞動就可以削減我們的困惑。懶惰只會讓事情舉步維艱，勤勞可以讓事情輕而易舉，這也是窮理查的話。他還說，起床晚的人，需要忙碌奔波一整天，到了深夜，工作還是做不完。懶惰走得實在太慢，貧窮很快就會超過它。正如我們在窮理查曆書裡讀到的（他補充說明的），掌控你的工作，而不是被你的工作驅使；還有，早睡早起，令人健康、富足、聰明。」

「所以，只是迫切地盼望好日子來有什麼用？想要過好日子，我們必須發憤圖強，自己爭取。正如窮理查所說：如果勤奮行事，不必向天求取；只是依靠希望活著的人，死得也快。不付出辛勞，哪裡有收穫；自己動手，才可以豐衣足食，因為我沒有土地耕種，就算我有，要交的稅也不輕。窮理查還有其他類似的箴言：有生意可以做的人，就會有錢賺；有事情可以做的人，不愁名利。但是生意也要用心經營，工作也要謹慎對待，否則到了最後，財產和房子變現抵押也不夠我們交稅。

「只要辛勤勞作，就不會挨餓；因為正如窮理查所說：勤奮工作的人，飢餓只敢探頭看，不敢進家門。就連庭吏和警察也無法進門，因為窮理查說過，勤勞償付債務，絕望只會更少。」

「即使你沒有找到寶藏，也沒有大筆遺產可以繼承，但勤奮卻是好運之母，這也是窮理查說的。他還說，上帝把所有的東西都賜給勤奮。懶漢沉睡你深耕，種出糧食賣得錢；今天的工作今天做，因為你不知道明天會有什麼阻礙等著你。所以窮理查說：今天價值兩個明天；還有，明天有事要做，今天就要著手。」

「你如果是一個僕人，被主人逮到偷懶的時候，你難道不會感到羞恥嗎？如果你是自己的主人，被自己逮到偷懶的時候，你難道不會感到羞恥嗎？這也是窮理查的話。窮理查還說，你必須要為自己、為家庭、為國家，以及你仁慈的君主負起責任的時候，黎明破曉，你就要起身行事；不要讓太陽看著你說：瞧啊，他還在躺著，真是不知羞恥啊！使用工具的時候，不必戴手套；不要忘記，戴手套的貓抓不到老鼠。確實，要做的事情有很多，而且你可能手腳也不夠靈活，但請你還是堅持下去，最後一定會得到好結果，因為水滴石穿，老鼠用牙齒也可以把粗繩了咬成兩半！斧頭雖小，卻可以砍倒大樹，這也是窮理查在曆書裡說過的，具體是哪一年，我現在不記得了。」

「我想，我聽到你們之中有人說：『難道一個人不能有空閒時間嗎？』我會告訴你，我的朋友，窮理查的話是：如果你想要多一些閒暇，就要善加利用自己的時間；還有，既然你連一分鐘也無法把握，更不應該隨便浪費一個小時。閒暇時間是為了做有意義的事情，所以勤奮的人會獲得這份閒適，懶惰的人卻從來不會獲得。因此，窮理查就說，閒適的生活跟懶散的生活完全是兩回事。難道你覺得偷懶會比勞動更讓你舒適嗎？不可能，因為窮理查說：煩惱源於無所事事的狀態，不必要的苦惱也會帶來繁重的辛勞。很多不勞動的人，只會依靠耍小聰明過日子，如果聰明不足，就會面臨破產。辛勤勞作可以讓人過得舒適，生活富足又受人尊敬：放飛快樂，快樂就會跟著你。勤快的紡紗機轉得快也織得多；現在，我有了羊和牛，每個人都會向我道早安；這些都是窮理查的諄諄教導。」

「但是有了勤勞，我們還要沉著、穩重、考慮周全，必須用眼睛仔細審視自己做的事情，絕對不能過於信任別人；因為，正如窮理查所說：我從來沒有見過一棵樹，被人們隨意移植，最後還可以比那些向下扎根的樹更加枝繁葉茂。」

「還有就是，搬家三次的危害相當於失火一次；顧好自己的店鋪，自己的店鋪也會顧好你；如果想要把自己的生意做好，那就去做吧；如果不想，就把它送給別人吧！想要依靠犁頭發達的人，要麼握住犁頭，要麼駕著犁頭。」

「還有，主人幹活，用的是眼睛，而不是手；還有，疏忽大意比缺乏知識的危害更大；還有，不盯著工人幹活，就是把你的錢包打開。過於信任別人的看顧，毀掉了很多人；但是如果可以自己看顧，卻是大有裨益的；因為，窮迪克說：知識之於好學者，就如財富之於細心者；權力之於膽大者，就如天堂之於有德者。還有，如果你想要有一個對自己忠誠、順從自己心意的僕人隨侍左右，你只能給自己當僕人。還有，迪克告誡你，再小的事情也要謹慎小心，因為有時候一個微小的疏忽會造成巨大的損失（譯者注：一著不慎，滿盤皆輸）。補充一點：缺了一顆釘子，會弄丟一隻馬掌；少了一隻馬掌，會失去一匹馬；失去一匹馬，會損失一個騎兵。最後，你會因為缺了一顆釘子而全軍覆沒。」

「我的朋友們，關於勤勞，我就說這麼多了，現在應該把注意力放在自己的事務上；但是，如果我們想要依靠自己的勤勞獲得實在的成功，我們還要把「節儉」加進去。如果一個人不懂得如何節省自己獲得的東西，他就會勞苦一輩子，最後處於身無分文的悲慘境遇。正如窮理查所說：廚房美味多，意志變薄弱；還有，自從女人們只顧著喝茶聊天，不管紡線織布，男人們也只顧著喝酒（譯者注：此處為潘趣酒）打牌，不再上山砍柴，很多錢財就被花在享用上。」

「如果你想要變得富有，他在另一本曆書裡說，儲蓄和收入都要同時考慮。印度群島沒有讓西班牙變得富有，原因是她（譯者注：代指西班牙）的支出大於收入。現在就改掉你那些鋪張浪費的愚蠢習慣，這樣你就不會每天都在抱怨世道艱難，賦稅繁重，家庭開銷很大；因為，正如窮理查所說，女人和紅酒，遊戲（譯者注：偏義副詞，喻指賭博）和欺詐，讓財富變少，欲望加深。還有，讓惡習得以繼續存活，還會生出兩個惡習。你可能會這樣想，喝一點茶或是一點潘趣酒，偶爾吃一頓貴的，穿一些好的，偶爾娛樂一下，這些是無傷大雅的事情；但是請記住窮理查的話：積少也可以成多；還有，要注意小筆開銷；小漏洞也可以讓大船沉沒；還有，誰要是貪戀珍饈美食，不久就會淪落街頭成為乞丐；還有，愚人籌辦盛宴，智者享用盛宴。」

「今天，為了參加這場擺滿各式華麗衣服和琳琅飾品的拍賣盛宴，你們在此地聚集。這些你們稱為貨物的東西，稍有不慎，它們就會變成邪惡的所在。你們只是想著拍賣的時候可以低價買進，或是買到物超所值的東西；但是如果買來以後卻沒有用武之地，它們對你來說就是買貴了。記住窮理查說的話，買了你不需要的東西，不久以後，你就要賣掉自己需要的物品。還有，哪怕只是價值一便士的東西，購買之前也要想一想。他的意思是：東西便宜可能只是表面上看起來便宜，實際上並非如此；或是便宜貨，看起來便宜，但是最後卻會掏空你的錢包，給你帶來的壞處多於好處。在另一個地方，他說：很多人因為花錢買價值一便士的東西，最後弄得傾家蕩產。還有，窮理查說：花錢之後買來的是後悔，這樣的愚蠢戲碼，因為不將曆書的忠告放在心上，幾乎每天都會在拍賣會上上演。」

「有智慧的人，正如窮迪克所說，善於從別人的錯誤中吸取教訓，愚蠢的人只有犯錯以後才可以吸取教訓；但是，可以因為別人的失敗而學會謹慎，這樣的人是有福的。許多人為了穿華麗的衣服，只能餓著肚子，勒緊褲帶，甚至連累家人一起挨餓。正如窮理查所說，綾羅綢緞，紅紗羽絨，哄得妻子不發火。這些生活不需要的物品不能稱為必需品，也很少被叫做生活便利品，只是因為它們外表漂亮，就有很多人趨之若鶩。就這樣，人類的『假需求』變得比『自然需求』更多；所以，正如窮迪克所說：對一個窮人來說，一窮百樣窮。對揮霍無度的人來說，貴紳也會淪為窮漢，最後不得不向他們曾經看不起的人請求接濟；自始至終勤勞節儉的人，自始至終都可以養活自己；在這種情況下，我們可以很清楚地看到，雙腿站立的農民比雙膝跪地的紳士更高貴，這也是窮理查的話。」

「或許他們有祖輩留下的綿薄遺產，但是他們自己很清楚，以自己的能力無法賺到這些錢；他們認為，只會有白天，不會有黑夜；所以，那麼多的錢，花一點出去不必放在心上（正如窮理查所說，小孩和傻瓜概念裡的二十先令，二十年也花不完），但是如果只是從米缸裡往外舀糧卻從來不添糧進去，不久之後，米缸就會看到底了。所以，正如窮迪克所說：不到井乾涸，不知水珍貴。但是如果他們及早接受窮理查的忠告，他們應該早就明白這一點。你如果想要知道金錢的真正價值，現在就去向別人借一些；因為，向別人借錢的人會遭遇傷心難堪；借錢給這種人的債主，他去討債的時候，還會將欠債的人推向悲傷的境地。窮迪克還建議，只是想著穿衣打扮，這是一個不幸；想要滿足自己的幻想，先問問自己的錢包。」

「還有，驕傲自負就像乞丐高聲乞討，只會更顯粗俗。你買到一件好東西的時候，一定還會買進十件其他的，但是你卻表現得好像只買了一件東西。但是窮迪克說，先起的欲望容易壓制，後來的欲望難以滿足。窮人要跟富人攀比，就像青蛙鼓起肚子想要跟公牛一樣大，都是愚不可及的。家大業大可以多冒風險，小船小舟應該靠岸行駛。」

「但是，驕傲之舉很快就會受到懲罰；因為正如窮理查所說，驕傲中午吃的是名為虛榮的飯，晚上喝的是叫做蔑視的湯。在另一個地方，窮理查還說，驕傲早餐吃的是富足，午餐吃的是貧窮，晚餐吃的是臭名。所以，究其原因，擺出自負的樣子到底有什麼用？還要冒這麼多風險，受這麼多罪？它既不能提升健康狀況，也不能減輕病痛折磨，更不能增加一個人的優點，只會製造嫉妒，加劇不幸。」

「蝴蝶到底是什麼？只是穿上花衣又化妝的毛毛蟲。花花公子只是徒有其表的傢伙，窮理查如是說。」

「但是，為了一些多餘無用的東西而背負債務，這是多麼瘋狂的一件事情。在今天的拍賣會上，我們被授予六個月賒購物品的優越權，這可能會使得我們之中的一些人加入拍賣的爭奪中，就是因為現在沒有現錢可以用，所以我們會覺得現在這樣沒有錢也很好（譯者注：因為有賒購的優越權在引誘）。然而，還是想想你身負重債應該怎麼辦吧！你只是在自己的自由上多設下一個限制。如果你無法及時償清，你會羞於見到你的債主，跟他說話也會心生畏懼；你還會編出一些可憐的藉口企圖矇混過關，逐漸地，你就會變得沒有信用，並且最終墮入謊言的深淵。因為，正如窮理查所說，萬惡之首是負債，其次是說謊。再者，出於同樣的目的，說謊騎在債務的背上。一個生來自由的英國人，不應該因為見到任何人或是與任何人說話而感到害羞或害怕。但是，貧窮經常剝奪一個人所有的精神和美德：空袋子，難立直。窮理查確實這樣說。」

「如果一個國家的君主或是政府頒布法令，禁止你打扮得像一個紳士或淑女，否則就會遭受牢獄之苦或是奴役之痛，你會怎麼想？你難道不會說你是自由的，有權利按照自己的喜好穿著打扮，這樣的法令實際上剝奪你的權利，這樣的政府就是專制？但是，你負債經營的時候，實際上已經將自己置於暴政之下！如果你無法償還債款，你的債主就有權利按照他的喜好來剝奪你的自由，他會因此限制你的生活目標，或是將你賣作奴僕！你跟債主討價還價得到優惠以後，或許很少想起有債要還這件事情；但是放債的人，窮理查也告訴我們，記性永遠比欠債的人好；他也在另一個地方說，放債的人就像身處某個神秘的宗教組織，對設定的日期盯得很緊，分秒不漏。」

「在你反應過來之前，催債的日子就到了；你要還的錢還沒有準備好，敲門聲就響了。或是，如果心裡記得要還債，開始的時候覺得期限很長，但是這個期限會慢慢變短，最後眼看就到了。時間就像在自己的腳上插了翅膀，也在自己的肩上插了翅膀，飛快流逝，一晃即過。窮理查說，那些借短期債的人，欠的錢應該在復活節還清。然後，他還說，借錢的人是放貸人的奴隸，負債者是債主的奴隸；所以，要蔑視枷鎖，捍衛自由，保持自我的獨立。勤勞就是自由，節儉也是自由。也許現在你覺得自己意氣風發，財運亨通，所以稍微揮霍也無傷大雅；但是不要忘記：年齡和需求，盡可能節省；早晨的太陽，轉瞬即逝。」

「正如窮理查所說，收入可能不確定也不恆常，但是只要你還活著，一定會有花銷，而且是源源不絕的。所以，窮理查說：建造兩個煙囪比讓一個煙囪經常冒煙更容易。因此，寧願空著肚子上床睡覺，也不要身負重債而醒來。賺取你可以賺到的，賺來的也要守住；這是讓你點石成金的魔法石，正如窮理查所說：獲得點金石以後，你就不會再抱怨時運不濟，或是賦稅沉重。這條守則，我的朋友，就是理性和智慧。但是，也不要過於依賴你的勤奮、節儉、謹慎，儘管這些是好東西，如果沒有上天的保佑，這些都會枯萎；所以，謙卑地祈求上天保佑，不要刻薄地對待沒有這種福氣的人，而是要安慰他們，幫助他們。要記住：約伯也曾經受苦，之後才會興旺富足。」

「現在，是時候總結了：經驗是一所收費昂貴的學校，但是愚蠢的人一定要進來學習。因為確實，我們可以給別人忠告，卻無法給他們行動，就像窮理查說的。但是，也不要忘記，如果聽不進勸告，誰來了也幫不上忙，這也是窮理查說的。還有，如果你不聽理性的話，她就會打斷你的手，讓你吃一些苦頭。」

就這樣，這位老先生結束他的長篇大論。人們聽完以後，心中深以為然，但是卻反其道而行，彷彿這只是一場人們已經習以為常的布道。因為拍賣開始以後，人們爭先恐後地大肆揮霍，不顧他的警告，也完全沒有對賦稅的擔心。我發現這位好人（譯者注：亞伯拉罕神父）將我的曆書研究得很透徹，消化吸收我二十五年以來所寫的每個主題的點點滴滴。他不厭其煩地提及我的名號，一定已經讓周圍的人很不耐煩，但是我的虛榮心卻因此得到極大的滿足。儘管我心裡也明白，他剛才演講提到的那些智慧之言，只有不到十分之一是我寫的，剩下的都是我從各個時代其他民族的思想寶庫裡挑選出來的智慧珍寶，但是他將功勞全部歸到我的身上。然而，我自己也下定決心，要躬身踐行這些智慧箴言，所以儘管我早有打算，想要換一件新外套，最後我還是改變初衷，選擇繼續穿舊外套。讀者，如果您也可以這樣做，我相信您收穫的利益也會跟我一樣多。

我是永遠為您效力的朋友，
理查・桑德斯
1757年7月7日一個謀士勝過兩個勇士。

One Nestor is worth two Ajaxes.

作為砧板，要穩固安靜；作為錘子，須敲擊有力。

When you're an Anvil, hold you still; when you're a Hammer, strike your Fill.

兩個騙子背叛彼此，不必責備其中一個，也用不著同情另一個。

When Knaves betray each other, one can scarce be blamed, or the other pitied.

小錯小罪，犯得習慣；大錯死罪，不日到來。

He that carries a small Crime easily, will carry it on when it comes to be an Ox.

湯姆整天都很快樂，從來看不到自己背著的煩惱。

Happy Tom Crump, ne'er sees his own Hump.

傻瓜最需要忠告，忠告卻只對智者更好。

Fools need Advice most, but wise Men only are the better for it.

沉默寡言不總是象徵智慧，喋喋不休卻總是代表愚蠢。

Silence is not always a Sign of Wisdom, but Babbling is ever a Mark of Folly.

偉大的謙遜背後藏著偉大的優點。

Great Modesty often hides great Merit.

你可以拖延，時間卻不會。

You may delay, but Time will not.

美德未必總是可以為你臉上增光，惡習卻一定可以讓你面目可憎。

Virtue may not always make a Face handsome, but Vice will certainly make it ugly.

揮霍時間讓你思想和物資都匱乏。

Prodigality of Time, produces Poverty of Mind as well as of Estate.

學會滿足等於擁有魔法石，可以點物成金。

Content is the Philosopher's Stone, that turns all it touches into Gold.

知足者心足物也足，抱怨者話多事也多。

He that's content, hath enough; He that complains, has too much.

驕傲自負坐進馬車（四輪大馬車）裡，羞愧恥辱排山倒海來。

Pride gets into the Coach, and Shame mounts behind.

出版業犯下的第一個錯誤就是「進入」。（譯者注：進入出版業）

The first Mistake in publick Business, is the going into it.

真相的一半，就是一個巨大的謊言。

Half the Truth is often a great Lie.

吃得太飽會使頭腦遲鈍：靈感繆斯會在廚房挨餓。（譯者注：吃得太

飽，不利於靈感的湧現）

A full Belly makes a dull Brain: The Muses starve in a Cook's Shop.

省錢之後有錢，勝過花錢之後討錢。

Spare and have is better than spend and crave.

善念如風，哪裡聽見哪裡流動。

Good-Will, like the Wind, floweth where it listeth.

蜂蜜雖然甜，蜜蜂卻有刺。

The Honey is sweet, but the Bee has a Sting.

在一個腐朽墮落的時代，強迫世界恢復秩序反而會引發混戰，不如自己顧好自己。

In a corrupt Age, the putting the World in order would breed Confusion; then e'en mind your own Business.

想要服務大眾，又想要取悅所有人，這是不切實際的。

To serve the Publick faithfully, and at the same time please it entirely, is impracticable.

當代的學識看不起古代的學問：就像現在的老師被學生嘲笑一樣。

Proud Modern Learning despises the antient: School-men are now laught at by School-boys.

人們經常誤解自己，卻很少忘記自己。

Men often mistake themselves, seldom forget themselves.

遊手好閒的人是魔鬼的傭人：穿著破爛不堪，吃食極度缺乏，報酬卻

是疾病。（譯者注：懶人容易墮落，以至於吃不飽，穿不暖，最後還有病來磨）

The idle Man is the Devil's Hireling; whose Livery is Rags, whose Diet and Wages are Famine and Diseases.

不能搶劫上帝或是窮人，除非你想要自取滅亡；老鷹從祭壇裡抓了一塊炭，最後燒掉自己的窩。（譯者注：多行不義必自斃）

Rob not God, nor the Poor, lest thou ruin thyself; the Eagle snatcht a Coal from the Altar, but it fired her Nest.

這一年，在一波又一波的歡呼聲中，結束。

With bounteous Cheer, Conclude the Year.

心學堂 16

窮理查的智慧
Poor Richard's Almanack

作者 班傑明・富蘭克林
譯者 王奕偉
美術構成 騾賴耙工作室
封面設計 九角文化/設計
發行人 羅清維
企劃執行 張緯倫、林義傑
責任行政 陳淑貞

企劃出版 海鷹文化
出版登記 行政院新聞局局版北市業字第780號
發行部 台北市信義區林口街54-4號1樓
電話 02-2727-3008
傳真 02-2727-0603
E-mail seadove.book@msa.hinet.net

總經銷 知遠文化事業有限公司
地址 新北市深坑區北深路三段155巷25號5樓
電話 02-2664-8800
傳真 02-2664-8801
網址 www.booknews.com.tw

香港總經銷 和平圖書有限公司
地址 香港柴灣嘉業街12號百樂門大廈17樓
電話 （852）2804-6687
傳真 （852）2804-6409

CVS總代理 美璟文化有限公司
電話 02-2723-9968
E-mail net@uth.com.tw

出版日期 2022年06月01日 一版一刷
2022年07月05日 一版五刷
定價 350元
郵政劃撥 18989626 戶名：海鴿文化出版圖書有限公司

國家圖書館出版品預行編目（CIP）資料

窮理查的智慧 ／ 班傑明・富蘭克林作 ； 王奕偉譯.
-- 一版. -- 臺北市 ： 海鴿文化，2022.06
面 ； 公分. --（心學堂；16）
ISBN 978-986-392-456-2（平裝）

1. 格言

192.8 111006254